REGENTS CRITICS SERIES

General Editor: Paul A. Olson

# LITERARY CRITICISM OF SAINTE-BEUVE

Other volumes in the Regents Critics Series are:

# Literary Criticism of Sainte-Beuve

*Translated and edited by*

EMERSON R. MARKS

UNIVERSITY OF NEBRASKA PRESS · LINCOLN

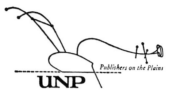

Publishers on the Plains

UNP

MANUFACTURED IN THE UNITED STATES OF AMERICA

To Bob and Anne

# Regents Critics Series

The Regents Critics Series provides reading texts of significant literary critics in the Western tradition. The series treats criticism as a useful tool: an introduction to the critic's own poetry and prose if he is a poet or novelist, an introduction to other work in his day if he is more judge than creator. Nowhere is criticism regarded as an end in itself but as what it is—a means to the understanding of the language of art as it has existed and been understood in various periods and societies.

Each volume includes a scholarly introduction which describes how the work collected came to be written, and suggests its uses. All texts are edited in the most conservative fashion consonant with the production of a good reading text; and all translated texts observe the dictum that the letter gives life and the spirit kills when a technical or rigorous passage is being put into English. Other types of passages may be more freely treated. Footnoting and other scholarly paraphernalia are restricted to the essential minimum. Such features as a bibliographical checklist or an index are carried where they are appropriate to the work in hand. If a volume is the first collection of the author's critical writing, this is noted in the bibliographical data.

PAUL A. OLSON

*University of Nebraska*

# Contents

# Introduction

## I

Born posthumously on December 23, 1804, at Boulogne-sur-Mer, Charles-Augustin Sainte-Beuve was raised by his mother, then aged forty, and a paternal aunt. As a preparation for a literary life his education was on the whole better than that enjoyed by most critics born in humble circumstances. By early adolescence he had learned his Latin classics at a local *pension* and was composing fluent Latin prose. In 1818 he moved to Paris, where he continued his literary studies, including Greek, first at the Lycée Charlemagne, then at the Collège Bourbon. He also attended the evening lectures on philosophy and science given at the Athénée.

Sainte-Beuve's first choice of a career was not literature, however, but medicine, for which he prepared at the Ecole de Médecine from 1823 to 1827. But he gradually gave it up for his true calling, encouraged first by the opportunity to contribute articles to the *Globe*, a literary review founded in 1824 by his teacher of rhetoric, Paul Dubois, then by the memorable meeting in 1827 with Victor Hugo, just after the appearance of his review of that rising young poet's *Odes et ballades* in the *Globe*. In the following year his first book, *Tableau historique de la poésie française et du théâtre français au XVI^e siècle*, appeared. The literary journalism that marked his debut continued well into the 1840s, as Sainte-Beuve contributed essays to the *Revue de Paris*, the newly founded *Revue des Deux Mondes*, and the *National*. The best of these critiques, collected in the *Portraits littéraires*, *Portraits de femmes*, and *Portraits contemporains*, display an analytical skill that makes it easy for a reader to forget that during these early years their author aspired to fame primarily as a poet, and actually published three volumes of indifferent verse before reluctantly concluding that his bent was critical rather than creative. There was also the novel *Volupté*, a thinly veiled fictionalization of his tawdry affair with Hugo's wife, Adèle, published in 1834.

Sainte-Beuve, who never married, was so much the man of letters as to be hardly anything else. His biography does not make very exciting reading, the few notable events in his sixty-five-year life being memorable chiefly for "bibliographical" reasons. Thus his lectures at the University of Lausanne during 1837–38 yielded *Port-Royal;* the twenty-one lectures delivered at the University of Liège in Belgium from October, 1848, to June, 1849, were later published as *Chateaubriand et son groupe littéraire sous l'Empire* (1861); the professorship of Latin poetry at the Collège de France, to which he was appointed in 1854 but which he abandoned after the second lecture, hissed off the podium by the students, bore fruit as *Etude sur Virgile* in 1857. The academic fiasco at the collège did not prevent his occupancy, from 1857 to 1861, of a chair of French literature at the Ecole Normale Supérieure. But Sainte-Beuve, we are told, was a poor lecturer, his delivery never effective, sometimes hardly audible. In 1865 he was created a member of Napoleon III's tame Imperial Senate, where, however, he had the courage to speak in defense of free thought and expression. He died in Paris on October 13, 1869.

In the whole roster of major literary critics it would be hard to find Sainte-Beuve's superior in learning or industry. His published works comprise over fifty volumes, the product of wide reading not only in *belles lettres* but also in history, biography, philosophy, theology, and virtually every other humanistic discipline. Even the most indefatigable modern scholar must admire the psychic energy and intellectual wealth that could produce the twenty-eight volumes of *Causeries du lundi* and *Nouveaux lundis*, that is, a twenty-page critical essay every week for about twenty years (1849–69), with only a few brief intermissions, on topics ranging from the Greeks to Flaubert. It was Louis Véron, managing editor of *Le Constitutionnel*, who invited Sainte-Beuve, then just back from Belgium and more or less at loose ends, to write a critical article to appear each Monday in that newspaper. Sainte-Beuve, after some understandable hesitation, agreed, though he later changed successively to two rival papers, *Le Moniteur* and *Le Temps*. That there was a sufficient audience for such serious literary discussion among newspaper readers certainly speaks well of the general cultural level of mid-nineteenth-century Parisians. In London at that time such a project would have been highly dubious; in Boston or New York it would have been unthinkable.

Sainte-Beuve combined a curiosity that let nothing escape his inspection with a flair for factual accuracy. Distrustful of the printed report, he would dispatch his manservant to the public library, during the composition of a *Lundi*, to verify the marriage date or precise ancestry of some obscure nobleman to whom he was making passing reference. Yet this concern for details never resulted in pedantry, never blurred his vision of the total picture they formed or weakened his grasp of broad intellectual movements or the essential character of historical periods.

Nowhere in his writings is this intellectual control more clearly apparent than in the six packed volumes of *Port-Royal*—that history that is so much more than history—on which he labored for two decades in the face of various personal and professional distractions. In Professor Wellek's judgment, "*Port-Royal* remains a triumph of intellectual historiography," its disunity of method and aim offset "by a unifying spirit that is the historical spirit at its best."[1] To read it through is certainly an unusual literary experience because *Port-Royal* is, so to speak, a work of documented imagination, a piece of meticulous scholarship that is also a kind of intellectual epic. In it are traced the fortunes of the Jansenist religious community from the time of its foundation in the early seventeenth century, at Port-Royal des Champs, a few miles south of Paris, to its final condemnation and physical demolition by papal and royal decrees a century later. The pace is leisurely, with time for full-length portraits of the inspired women, the scholarly and dedicated priests, and the well-born laymen who gladly sacrificed brilliant social and professional careers for the life of solitude, privation, and meditation in a rural monastery. All this is varied and enriched by digressions into social history, theology, and literary criticism. What makes so much of this long and detailed work still such absorbing reading is that Sainte-Beuve conceived his subject poetically, in the form of a grand

1. René Wellek, *The Age of Transition*, vol. 3 of *A History of Modern Criticism 1750–1950* (New Haven: Yale University Press, 1965), pp. 44, 45.

drama, as he tells us in the Preliminary Discourse. His *Port-Royal* is not merely that religious order whose activities form an especially piquant chapter in the religious history of France. It is that *Port-Royal* so beloved of its own ("Ce Port-Royal tant aimé des siens ..."), with Pascal for its champion and Racine for its pupil, fit subject enough for a literary critic.

To the rich and often turbulent French intellectual life that spanned the reigns of the two Napoleons, Sainte-Beuve contributed as poet, novelist, historian, academician, and politician. But always and in everything he was the critic, and it is as such that he is exclusively represented in this anthology.

## II

The appearance of a new translation of Sainte-Beuve's criticism a century after his death is an appropriate occasion for both a glance at his posthumous reputation, especially in the English-speaking world, and a fresh evaluation of his achievement. The latter is a more difficult task than is usual in such cases because no other leading critic has been at first so idolatrously praised and then so scornfully denounced as Sainte-Beuve. Before World War I, the chorus of acclaim was supported by the more telling tribute of his widespread influence, just as since then occasional denunciation has been accompanied by the worse damnation of general neglect. When Marcel Proust's notorious attack was first made public in 1954, it added weight to objections that had been raised earlier by others. One was Sainte-Beuve's obvious blindness to the merits of such great contemporaries as Balzac, Stendhal, and Baudelaire. Another was the deficient aesthetic sense that often led him to relish a book of memoirs above a book of poems. There was also the graver charge that he tended to confuse a literary product with its producer. To know a book, to know it thoroughly, Sainte-Beuve thought, a critic must scrutinize every scrap of information about the author's beliefs, habits, experiences, heredity, and associates, from which he might construct an accurate psychological portrait. But, Proust objected, this procedure overlooks the fact that "a book is the product of a different *self* from the self we manifest in our habits, in our social life, in our vices."[2] Sainte-Beuve thus stood convicted of what modern British and American critics have deplored as the "personal heresy." We are therefore not surprised to find Professors Wimsatt and Brooks granting him hardly more than a single page in a history of literary criticism which contains a full and generous treatment of Matthew Arnold.[3]

Yet if we are not surprised, Arnold himself, who regarded his distinguished French contemporary as the literary critic par excellence, surely would have been. So would several later writers, notably some in the United States. So gifted a judge as Henry James admired the comprehensiveness and complete freedom from vulgarity in Sainte-Beuve's literary evaluations, which Lafcadio Hearn less moderately pronounced nearly infallible. Perhaps Hearn, from whom Sainte-Beuve is simply "the greatest critic who ever lived,"[4] is a witness somewhat discredited by his verbal extravagance. But this objection hardly holds against the way Sainte-Beuve withstood the tougher-minded scrutiny of Irving Babbitt and Paul Elmer More. The "writer of the incomparable *Lundis*," More called him—those *Lundis* on which he modelled his own *Shelburne Essays*. "I do not know how it affects others," he wrote in one of these, "but for me, as I look at the long row of volumes which hold the interpretation of French literature, I am almost overwhelmed at the magnitude of this man's achievement."[5]

The variety and range of Sainte-Beuve's criticism, even his very inconsistencies, have tended to make him all things to all men. The critic whose grave reservations about romantic writers endeared him to the antiromantic Babbitt and More was praised as a dogma-free impressionist by Joel Elias Spingarn at a moment (1922) when Spingarn was the American spokesman for what he took to be the

2. "Contre Sainte-Beuve," in *Marcel Proust on Art and Literature 1896–1919*, translated by Sylvia Townsend Warner (New York: Meridian Books, 1958), pp. 99–100.

3. William K. Wimsatt, Jr., and Cleanth Brooks, *Literary Criticism: A Short History* (New York: Alfred A. Knopf, 1957).

4. Quoted in Robert Mahieu, *Sainte-Beuve aux Etats-Unis* (Princeton: Princeton University Press, 1945), p. 105.

5. "The Centenary of Sainte-Beuve," in *Shelburne Essays*, 3d ser. (New York: Houghton Mifflin Co., 1905), p. 77.

impressionist aesthetics of Benedetto Croce. For Sainte-Beuve's younger countryman Hippolyte Taine (among others), his distinctive excellence was as a "scientific" critic, the "natural historian of minds," whereas a twentieth-century compatriot, Victor Giraud, has argued that the true and valuable Sainte-Beuve is more nearly dilettante than scientist. Critics in our own time and country, especially those whose literary taste and doctrines owe most to T. S. Eliot, have found little or nothing to commend in the *Portraits* and the *Lundis*. Yet Eliot himself once called Sainte-Beuve a critic of genius.

The list of contradictory or contrasting estimates of Sainte-Beuve is a long one, starting during his lifetime and still in progress. No one who reads him—reads enough of him—is likely to ascribe this phenomenon entirely to careless or prepossessed interpretation. The plain fact, whether for exasperation or approval, is that in method, aim, theoretical premise, and sometimes (though more rarely) even in taste, there is not one Sainte-Beuve but several. Inconsistency and self-contradiction are therefore inevitable, and the occasional efforts of his admirers to contain him in some formula expressive of a complex or multi-leveled unity never quite succeed. Some part of him always escapes. The observation of a recent historian of French literary criticism that Sainte-Beuve's critical *manner* tends toward impressionism while his critical *method* tends toward the scientific[6] has a certain aphoristic validity. Yet how much of the author of the *Causeries de lundi* alone, even of his manner and method, does it belie!

What should in fairness be noted is that his protean quality is at least consistent with the conception of the critical spirit which Sainte-Beuve adopted and advocated early in his career and never altered. If he has been "all things to all men," that may be because he once described the critic's role in exactly that phrase. Critics, he argued in "On Bayle and the Critical Spirit" (1835), willingly take all sides of a question and even "count it no fault to refute themselves and subvert their own thinking." So abandoned an impressionism (Sainte-Beuve's critic is as "characterless" as Keats's chameleonlike poet) may seem to leave no room at all for the critic's traditional office as judge, and in fact Sainte-Beuve was later forced to answer

6. Pierre Moreau, *La Critique littéraire en France* (Paris, 1960), p. 123.

the charge of evading judgment. Though this charge was demonstrably unfounded, it is nonetheless true that he always felt it a more congenial task to understand a piece of literature, to grasp and describe its unique quality, than to determine its rank in some scale of literary value. But this description, to be successful, requires in the critic a generous portion of that "sympathetic imagination" which in English criticism is best evinced in the essays and lectures of Charles Lamb and William Hazlitt. Admittedly, a critic runs risks in such self-abandonment to the object of his examination, especially the risk of producing only a parodic paraphrase of his author, as Sainte-Beuve was well aware. Nonetheless, he adhered throughout his life to the belief that a critic must always "dip his pen into the inkwell of the author he wishes to describe"—surely a formulation as daring as the most thoroughgoing impressionist could ask for.

Sainte-Beuve's celebrated self-description as a natural historian of minds has been too hastily seized upon as a pretext for including him among such critical "scientists" as Taine and Ferdinand Brunetière. This is not to say that he entirely escaped—or could have escaped—the powerful lure of the triumphant scientism of his age, with its bright promise of being able to refer every phenomenon, whether of body or spirit, to a set of fixed determinants or causal laws, and thereby bring to every branch of human inquiry both the objectivity and the predictability of mathematical physics. In ebullient moments, this erstwhile medical student cannot help at least adopting the jargon of the reigning faith. "Tell me the state of a poet's health," he smugly declares, "and I'll tell you the overall tone, the quality, wholesome or sickly, of his writings." Yet rarely, if ever, did he attempt any such thing or even seem concerned to prove it possible. What the best and most characteristic of his critical practice bears out instead is the sincerity of his persuasion that criticism is an art rather than a science: an art of "responding sensitively to works of genius and making them admired." Just as the poet depended on inspiration, Sainte-Beuve told his readers, so too did the critic, who alike had his muse, named *Enthusiasm*. If, as has been asserted, Sainte-Beuve moved in his last years toward a more naturalistic position, the change is not very noticeable in his

actual practice. He was of course to the end alert to new developments in his métier and frequently expressed his reactions to them.
A few years before his death, in 1864, he gave what can be taken as
his final view of the relationship between the critic's function and the
scientific and historical methods. "Literary criticism," he wrote,

> cannot become a pure science. It will remain an art, and, in the hands
> of those who have the skill to apply it, a very delicate art. But this art
> will profit, and has already profited, by all the inductions of science and
> all the acquisitions of history.

## III

When Sainte-Beuve wrote that literary study led him naturally to
moral study, he was not so much arguing a logical progression as
confessing a personal curiosity about the creative personality and the
creative process. In itself that curiosity cannot be legitimately
relegated to critical limbo by glibly labeling it the personal or
biographical heresy. Sainte-Beuve and his detractors are at one in
their insistence that all good criticism must begin—and perhaps
end—with a full and sensitive appreciation of a literary work as
such. But surely the fuller and more sensitive that appreciation is
in any given instance, the more natural and legitimate must be the
impulse to discover what in the man himself—his experience, his
work habits, his personal psychology—may account, if not for the
excellence, at any rate for the peculiar flavor and quality of his
creations. This kind of investigation is admittedly elusive and tricky,
more so perhaps than Sainte-Beuve was aware; moreover, it has
often proved least fruitful when applied to the very greatest artists,
who, as Arnold wrote of Shakespeare, seem not to "abide our
question." This limitation may in part explain Sainte-Beuve's undue
preoccupation with writers of the second rank about which some of
his readers have complained.

In our century a whole generation of critics and scholars have
thought and written under the guidance of T. S. Eliot's cogent pro-
nouncement that "the more perfect the artist, the more completely
separate in him will be the man who suffers and the mind which
creates." When they were first written, Eliot's words were a much
needed caveat, and they remain salutary. On the other hand it

would not seem frivolous to argue that the very raison d'être of literary biography is the assumption that at some profound and doubtless murky level of consciousness the suffering man and his creative mind are not entirely disjunct. (Eliot himself was later forced to concede "a particular relation between the two.")

In this connection, it is interesting to find Sainte-Beuve, in an essay on Pierre Corneille written as early as 1829, recording his delight in reading literary biographies. No other kind of literature, he thought, could be so absorbing or so profitable to the critic and the literary historian. He admired Samuel Johnson's *Lives of the English Poets* as well as Boswell's great biography of Johnson himself, and expressed regret that the art of literary biography had been less cultivated in France than in England and Germany.

The valid objection to Sainte-Beuve's literary portraiture is not that he confuses author and work, but that, in too many essays, he displays a greater interest in the author than in the work, and frequently in aspects of the author having little or nothing to do with his compositions. The reader is therefore forced to consume an intolerable deal of biographical sack with his halfpennyworth of critical bread. Yet Sainte-Beuve seldom forgets, in fact often underscores, not only the crucial distinction between poem and poet but also that further distinction between poet and man which Proust accused him of overlooking. The difference is that Proust would have critical attention focused on the poet exclusively, whereas Sainte-Beuve aimed at a multifaceted portrait of the whole personality. In the youthful essay on Corneille just mentioned, he inveighs against certain literary biographers who make the mistake of supposing that an author's whole biography can be inferred from his writings. To this mistake he ascribed the superficial criticism which failed to penetrate to the man behind the poet. The few occasions on which he himself neglects the distinction involve highly self-expressive, lyric poets like Alfred de Musset. For with a lyric poet, he wrote, "his lyre and his soul, his life and his work, are the same thing." From our twentieth-century perspective, we can easily identify this statement as an obvious form of the romantic myth of the poet. In less bemused moments Sainte-Beuve saw clearly enough that even good lyric verse, as he said of Théophile Gautier's, is never a direct outpouring of the poet's thoughts and emotions. His chief praise of Alfred de Vigny's elegies is that Vigny's tears, as he puts it, had undergone a metamorphosis in verbal representation. Similarly, he is careful to point out the subtle imaginative transfiguration to which Bernardin de Saint-Pierre subjected his personal experiences in the composition of the novel *Paul et Virginie*.

The unconscious metonymy by which we ask someone whether he enjoys "Yeats," when we mean "Yeats's poetry," is justified by the simple fact that a writer's literary style is in some sense an expression of his unique personality, of precisely that ingredient of his total self that belongs to the artist in him. This assumption is at least not open to the kind of protest rightly made against the attempt to infer a poet's love-life from his love poems, and it provides critical justification for the best of Sainte-Beuve's "psychography." In a late essay on Bishop Bossuet included in the second volume of the *Nouveaux lundis*, Sainte-Beuve gives us a "character" of the great pulpit orator. But his stated aim, "accurately to grasp the peculiar form of Bossuet's mind," is an *aesthetic* character, the analogue of Bossuet's eloquence. In an earlier *Lundi*, Saint-Beuve sees the clash between realistic and romantic elements in Lamartine's *Les Confidences* not in moral or psychological terms but rather as symptomatic of the poet's aesthetic unsteadiness. What is objectionable, he insists, is not any particular word Lamartine uses so much as his whole poetic vein, "which betokens a profound modification in the poet's way of seeing and feeling." Much the same nexus between style and personality is implied in T. S. Eliot's conception of poetic sensibility. Nor would it be extravagant to glimpse in Sainte-Beuve's notion an anticipation of the so-called existential method of more recent critics like Maurice Blanchôt and Jean-Pierre Richard.

Such affinities to the kinds of critical writing that are admired and practiced today may do much to commend Sainte-Beuve to modern readers. They would do even more if he had made it a practice to sustain his close analyses throughout whole essays. Unfortunately, the typical Sainte-Beuve essay consists of brief passages of critical appreciation separated by longer stretches of anecdote, broad comparative generalization, or biographical narrative.

Despite the catholicity of Sainte-Beuve's tastes and interests, the *Portraits* and *Lundis* are unified by certain recurrent attitudes and predilections that betray their common authorship. As already noted, he displayed from the outset a strange preference for writers not of the first rank. Worse still, there are many essays in which he devotes page after page to authors scarcely worth ranking at all, personages whose claim to attention was not literary so much as social, political, or military. Often, when he did turn to a literary giant, it was to spend more time on his juvenilia or other opuscula than on his acknowledged masterpieces.

As Sainte-Beuve grew older, his early preference for Attic grace and decorum, as against the sublime and the rhapsodic, became more marked. He experienced a growing disenchantment with the romantic school of Chateaubriand, Lamartine, Hugo, and their fellows, which at the start of his career he had celebrated with genuine though scrupulously qualified approval. Above all else he deplored what he regarded as the distinguishing feature of the romantic temperament: that pathology of the spirit known as romantic melancholy, *Weltschmerz*, or the *mal de René*, as Sainte-Beuve himself first encountered it, embodied in Chateaubriand's hypersensitive hero. It was, as he saw it, a disease epidemic in the nineteenth century; and it seems clear that his obsession with it owes much to his having once contracted it personally. Apparently it left scars. Sainte-Beuve's classicism, however, springs from sources far sounder than any mere quirk of his own temperament. It derives ultimately from the original classics—from the Greeks and from Horace and Virgil—and more immediately from the most per-durable elements of France's own classical tradition: Pascal's disillusioned conception of man, Voltaire's clarity of thought and expression, and the marble contours of Boileau's eminently civilized poetics.

A great deal of Sainte-Beuve can therefore be read as an anatomy of romanticism, written (since he was an active participant in its French beginnings) from within. Now and then the strength of his convictions seems to carry him to excess, as when he declares a liking for Lamartine's lovely poem "Le Lac" to be a sign of diseased taste. On the whole, however, his destructive analysis is informed by a clear-eyed recognition of the too frequent lapses into morbid self-absorption, sentimentalism, and emotional immaturity to which many romantic writers were prone.

Yet if Sainte-Beuve's own taste in literature was essentially classic, his distinctive contribution to criticism, the literary portrait, is an outgrowth of that stress on individualism and the cult of genius which are hallmarks of romanticism. As a literary critic he is therefore at once the censor and the child of his times.

*Note on the Text*

This translation is based on the following French texts: for "Madame de Sévigné's *Letters*," *Portraits de femmes* (Paris: Garnier Frères, 1886); for "Pascal's *Pensées*," *Port-Royal*, 7 vols., 3d ed. (Paris: Librairie de L. Hachette, 1867); for the *Lundi* essays, *Causeries du lundi*, 15 vols. (Paris: Garnier Frères, n.d.) and *Nouveaux lundis*, 13 vols., 7th ed. (Paris: Calmann Lévy, 1886–97); and for "Virgil and the Epic," *Etude sur Virgile* (Paris: Calmann Lévy, 1891). For all but two of the selections, "What Is a Classic?" and "On the Literary Tradition," I have supplied the titles and at the end of each selection given both its source and date of first publication. Deletions from the original texts are indicated by three asterisks (* * *). Except for those marked [Sainte-Beuve], the notes are my own. A few of Sainte-Beuve's notes, those that add little or nothing of interest to modern readers, have been silently omitted.

In order not to destroy their poetic quality for those who can read the languages, I have reproduced Sainte-Beuve's quotations of Latin and French verse in my text; translations of these are provided in the notes. I have done the same with the quotations from Chesterfield's French-language letters. For Sainte-Beuve's French versions of quotations from English authors, I have given the original English in place of what would have been an obviously pointless retranslation of my own.

Like most translators of prose, I have everywhere aimed at the strictest fidelity to the original that could be achieved in readable English. In the relatively few places where Sainte-Beuve's style makes this aim at all difficult, I consulted previous versions (where they exist), sometimes to advantage, sometimes not. In two places where I distrusted the accuracy of my own "Englishing," I am indebted for help to M. Pierre Vitoux of the Université de Montpellier, and to Miss Nilli Diengott of Wayne State University.

EMERSON R. MARKS

*University of Massachusetts—Boston*

# LITERARY CRITICISM OF
## SAINTE-BEUVE

# The Natural History of Minds:
# An Outline of a Critical Method

*In 1862 Sainte-Beuve took the occasion of a two-part causerie on Chateaubriand to meet the frequent objection that he lacked any consistent theory or method. The result is his most sustained exposition of naturalistic criticism. Books are the expressions of human beings. Literary study therefore goes beyond subjective and superficial appreciation to attain the objectivity and order of science only when the critic penetrates to the men behind the books, not only studying them in the uniqueness of their personal heredity and development but also assigning them to the moral classes and subclasses, the "families," to which they belong, by a method analogous to that used in botany. As Sainte-Beuve conceived it, however, the analogy is at best a loose one, which he never pressed very far in application. Here he seems to have intended both an apologia for the kind of literary portraiture he did so well and a conciliatory gesture to the science-oriented critical generation ascendant during his declining years.*

\* \* \* For me, literature, the production of an author, is not distinct or at any rate not separable from the rest of the man and his make-up. I can relish a work by itself, but I find it hard to judge it apart from a knowledge of the man who wrote it; I am quite willing to say, "As the tree is, so is its fruit." Quite naturally, therefore, literary study leads me to moral study.

With the ancient authors we lack sufficient means of observation. With the truly ancient, those of whom there remain only half-broken statues, we cannot in most cases turn to the author, book in hand. And so we have to be content with writing critical commentaries on his works and admiring them, while we try to guess at what the author or poet behind them was like. In this way we can

1

reconstruct the figures of poets or philosophers, busts of Plato, Sophocles, or Virgil, all highly idealized; nothing more is permitted by the incomplete state of our knowledge, the scarcity of sources, and the lack of any means of gathering information or recovering the facts. A mighty river, in most cases unfordable, divides us from the great men of antiquity. Let us salute them from the opposite bank.

With modern writers the situation is entirely different, and criticism, which adjusts its methods to the materials available, here has a different task to perform. To know, and know thoroughly, one more man, especially if that man is an individual of note, and famous, is an important function and by no means to be scorned.

The study of moral character is still at the elementary stage of compiling details and describing individuals, or at the very most a few species; Theophrastus and La Bruyère[1] did not take us beyond this stage. A day will come, which I think I have glimpsed in the course of my observations, when moral science will be established and the great families of minds and their principal divisions will be determined and known. When that day comes, once the main quality of a particular mind is known, it will be possible to deduce its several other qualities.[2] Of course, in studying men we shall never be able to proceed in quite the same way as in studying animals or plants. Human nature is more complex, endowed with what we call *liberty*, which in each case admits of a great variety of possible combinations. Still and all, I conceive that in the course of time the science of the moralist will be established on broader foundations; at present it has reached the point where botany was before Jussieu, or comparative anatomy before Cuvier,[3] the anecdotal stage, so to speak. We are simply compiling monographs, recording the details of observation; but I begin to make out links and relationships, and a more enlightened and comprehensive intellect with an acute sense

1. Theophrastus's *Characters*, upon which Jean de la Bruyère based *Les caractères* (1688), is a delineation of moral types.

2. "In characters there is a certain necessity, certain relationships, so that a given major trait implies secondary traits." Goethe, *Conversations with Eckermann*. [Sainte-Beuve]

3. Antoine Laurent de Jussieu's *Genera plantarum* (1789) founded modern botanic classification. Baron Cuvier's *Tableau élémentaire de l'histoire naturelle des animaux* (1798) first established a classification for animals.

for details will one day succeed in discovering the great natural divisions that correspond to the families of minds.

Yet even if the science of minds is developed to the point we can now imagine, it would always be so subtle and elusive that it would exist only for those who have a natural vocation and talent for close observation: it would always be an *art*, demanding a skilled artist, just as medicine requires medical tact in the practitioner, philosophy a philosophic bent in those who would be philosophers, and only a born poet should meddle with poetry.

I am therefore supposing a man gifted with a particular talent and facility for understanding the literary groups or families (since my concern at the moment is with literature); someone who can discern them almost at first glance and grasp their life and spirit, making it his vocation to do so because he is qualified in this vast field of human minds.

Let us assume we wish to study a man outstanding, or simply notable, for his productions, a writer whose works we have read and who merits thorough examination. How shall we go about it in such a way as to omit nothing about him that is essential or important, to go beyond the older rhetorical judgments, and (as little as possible taken in by words, phrases, and fine expressions of conventional sentiment) to penetrate to the truth as a scientist does in studying natural phenomena?

It is most helpful, right off, to begin at the beginning, and when the means are at hand, to consider the superior or distinguished writer in his native region and family background. A great deal of light can be thrown on the essential, underlying quality of minds by knowing their physiological ancestry; in most cases, however, those deeper roots remain concealed from our view. When we do know something about them our study is greatly enriched.

In at least some part of his nature, the man of genius is inevitably found reflected in his relatives, especially in his mother, that surest and most direct relative; but also in his sisters, his brothers, and even his children. In them we find those essential lineaments of character that are often masked in the great man himself because they are too condensed and intermingled. In his blood relations the essential quality is laid bare, and nature herself has done the analyzing for us. This is a very elusive notion which must be clarified by proper names and an array of particular facts. I shall point out a few.

Take sisters for example. This Chateaubriand I have been discussing[4] had a sister who, as he himself informs us, had a *vivid imagination combined with an underlying stupidity*, which must have bordered on sheer silliness. Another sister, entirely different, was the divine Lucille (the Amélie of his *René*), who had an exquisite sensibility, an imagination of the tender, melancholy kind, with nothing of what her brother had in his own temperament to balance or correct it. She went insane and killed herself. The ingredients that were united and collaboratively fused in him, at least in his creative gift, and kept in a kind of equilibrium, were disproportionately split between the two girls.

I have no personal knowledge of M. de Lamartine's sisters, but I have always remembered a chance remark by M. Royer-Collard, who had known them. He spoke of them in their first youth as of something charming and melodious, like a nest of nightingales. Balzac's sister, Madame Surville, who bears a striking physical resemblance to her brother, has the effect of giving a more favorable impression of him to those who, perhaps wrongly, are like myself something less than wholehearted admirers of the celebrated novelist, an impression that enlightens, reassures, and sets right. Beaumarchais's sister Julie, whom M. de Loménie has made known to us, perfectly reflects her brother's gay banter, his keen, unrestrained humor and irresistibly sparkling wit; she carried it to the very limits of decency if not sometimes beyond. This lively, amiable girl died almost with a song on her lips; she was indeed the sister of Figaro, formed from the same mold and material.[5]

It is the same with the brothers of a writer. The satirist Boileau had an elder brother equally satirical but rather dull and vulgar; another brother, a canon, was very gay, much given to repartee and

4. Earlier in the essay from which this excerpt is taken.

5. *Beaumarchais et son Temps*, by M. de Loménie. (See Vol. I, pp. 36–52.) [Sainte-Beuve]

Figaro is the resourceful protagonist of Beaumarchais's comedies *Le Barbier de Séville* (1775) and *Le Mariage de Figaro* (1784).

caprice, but a bit grotesque, too overdone and glaring. In Boileau himself nature had combined the qualities of the two others, but with sensitivity and discrimination, and then seasoned his entire temperament with a wit worthy of Horace. But to those who would doubt the fertility of Boileau's artistic resources, because they see in him a man of acquired culture but no natural poetic zest, it is useful to point out his personal environment and family connections.

Madame de Sévigné, as I have more than once remarked, seems to have been split in her two children: the *chevalier* volatile, heedless, elegant, and Madame de Grignan intelligent but somewhat lacking in warmth, having inherited reason as her share. Their mother had all these qualities. No one doubts her elegance, but some would deny her gravity and reason, and it is well to call their attention to Madame de Grignan, in whom reason alone predominated. Taken in conjunction with the evidence provided by her writings, this is a helpful guide.[6]

And in our own time have not certain daughters of poets now dead for some years helped me to a fuller understanding of their fathers? Sometimes I have thought I could rediscover in these women the enthusiastic warmth of soul and certain youthful paternal qualities in their simple unadulterated state, preserved, as it were, in their purest essence.

These examples should suffice to convey my idea without laboring the point. When the critic has obtained all the information he can about the descent and the immediate and proximate family of an eminent author, one essential point remains to be determined (next to his studies and education); and that is his earliest society, the group of friends and contemporaries he associated with at the moment his talent showed itself, when it first took on definite, mature form. It is a fact that a creative talent always bears the mark of this experience, a coloring which it never loses, whatever it may attempt in later years.

Let us be clear about what I mean by the word *group*, which I happen to be using deliberately. As I define it, a group is not a fortuitous and artificial collection of intellectuals banded together

6. Compare Sainte-Beuve's youthful essay on Madame de Sévigné's *Letters*, pp. 30–41 below.

for a common purpose, but the natural and more or less spontaneous
association of talented young minds, not exactly all alike and of the
same family, but of the same "brood" hatched in the same spring
under the same star, who share a sense of having been born, despite
differences of taste and aspiration, for a common enterprise. Such
was the little society formed by Boileau, Racine, La Fontaine, and
Molière around 1664, at the dawn of our literary golden age; they
represent the most perfect example of a literary group—all geniuses!
Then at the opening of the nineteenth century, in 1802, there was
the circle that included Chateaubriand, Fontanes, Joubert,[7] and
others, another such group which for its intellectual quality alone
we cannot dismiss as paltry. Then too—not to confine ourselves to
domestic cases—we have the group of young students and poets at
Göttingen in 1770 [1772], who published the *Muses' Almanack*:
Bürger, Voss, Hölty, Stolberg, and the rest.[8] We have yet another in
the group of critics at Edinburgh in 1800 [1802], headed by Jeffrey,
the group which gave rise to the celebrated *Review* over which he
presided.[9] Speaking of the association at the University of Dublin
which included the young Thomas Moore, a judicious critic has
written:

> Every time a collection of young people is animated by a liberal
> inspiration and feels called to great undertakings, it is always stirred
> and quickened by individual associations. The professor dispenses only
> dead knowledge from his chair; the living spirit, the spirit which will
> constitute the intellectual life of a people and a period, is to be found
> rather among these young enthusiasts who band together to share
> their discoveries, forebodings, and hopes.[10]

7. Like Chateaubriand, Louis Fontanes and Joseph Joubert represented the new
romantic idealism that supplanted the rationalism of the eighteenth century in
French literature.

8. These poets of the *Göttingener Musenalmanach* belong to the early "storm and
stress" phase of German romanticism, predominant from 1770 to 1790.

9. Francis Jeffrey, prestigious editor of the *Edinburgh Review* from 1803 to 1829,
is now best remembered for his harsh review of Wordsworth's *Excursion*. Others of
his group include his fellow contributors to the *Review*, the Reverend Sydney
Smith, its founder, Henry Brougham, and Archibald Constable.

10. M. Forcade, in the *Revue des Deux Mondes* for February, 1853. [Sainte-Beuve]

I need not cite examples of such literary groups from our own generation. Well known among others are the circle of critics who wrote for the *Globe* around 1827, the exclusively poetic group associated with *La Muse française* in 1824, and the Cénacle of 1828.[11] Not a single one of the talented people, all of whom were young at that time, emerged unaffected by his participation in one of these groups. This is why I say that a critic who would gain a thorough understanding of a talent does well to find out in what critical or poetic milieu it first took shape, to what literary group it naturally belongs, and then study it carefully in that setting. For therein lies its true beginning.

The very greatest individuals have no need of groups because they themselves are the nuclei around which the lesser figures gather. Still, it is the group, the association, the banding together in an active exchange of ideas and constant mutual emulation with his peers, which allows the man of talent to attain the fullest realization of his creative potential. Some writers participate in several groups at once, moving constantly from one cultural milieu to another, thereby perfecting, transforming, or distorting their art. In such cases it is essential that the critic not lose sight of the hidden spring or enduring driving force, which persists unchanged even amid successive metamorphoses and conversions gradual or sudden.

Examined in this fashion, restored to its historic frame of time and place, attended by all the circumstances surrounding its birth, each literary work reveals its full meaning, both historical and literary, and regains its rightful degree of originality, novelty, or derivativeness; and when the critic comes to judge the work he avoids the risks inevitably incurred by a purely rhetorical criticism of discovering imaginary beauties and expressing irrelevant admiration.

When I use the term *rhetorical* (which I do not intend in a completely unfavorable sense), I am by no means condemning judgments of taste or denying the value of a reader's immediate responses to a given work. I do not renounce Quintilian; I merely indicate the

11. The Cénacle, founded by Sainte-Beuve and Victor Hugo, was a group that also included Vigny, Musset, Mérimée, and the elder Dumas.

equally decisive to the critic who would grasp it whole. This is the moment when it begins to spoil, to fall off or deviate from its best. Put it in the kindest terms you wish, it happens to almost every author. I refrain from citing examples; but in most of the literary careers available for our inspection a point is reached where the expected maturity fails of attainment, or else, if it is attained, is overdone, and the excess of its very excellence becomes a flaw. Some writers become stiff and dried out; some go slack and lose control; others become callous and dull; a few turn sour. What was a smile has become a grimace. After the initial moment when a talent flourishes in the splendor of young manhood, we have to take account of this sad second crucial point, when it is debased and altered in the process of growing old.

Nowadays, one of the commonest ways of praising an aging author is to say to him, "Your talent was never more youthful." Such flattery should not be taken too seriously. Sooner or later the day comes when the years felt within begin to show outwardly. This process, we must nevertheless admit, varies greatly with the individual talent and the particular genre. Just as it is in war, so in poetry, drama, or whatever: some aspirants enjoy only a single day of glory, one brilliant hour, a unique victory for which their names are remembered and which none of their subsequent achievements can match. They are like Augereau, who would have done well to die the evening after Castiglione.[16] Others achieve many successes, in forms that vary and renew themselves with each year. Fifteen years is the usual length of a literary career. A few writers manage to double that, entering on or even completing a second career. There are those less inspired kinds of writing especially suited to old age, memoirs, recollections, criticism, or the kind of poetry that borders on prose. Elderly writers are well advised to stick to these types. Without taking too literally the precept *Solve senescentem . . . ,*[17] without quite putting his horse out to grass—which should be postponed as long as possible—the aging writer will lead him gently

16. Pierre Augereau was one of Napoleon's generals, who turned defeat to victory at the battle of Castiglione, in Italy, fought on August 5, 1796.
17. *Solve senescentem mature sanus equum.* [Be wise in time and dismiss the aging horse from service.] Horace *Epistles* 1. 1, line 8.

downhill by the bridle. This can, moreoever, make a very favorable impression. There are also rare cases of writers who after years of imperfect, sparse production seem to improve with old age, never before having appeared to such advantage. Take, for example, that amiable Swiss Voltaire, Bonstetten, or that one-quarter genius, Ducis.[18] But these men are exceptions to the rule.

A critic can hardly avail himself of too many means and methods for comprehending a man, by which I mean something more than a pure detached intellect. One cannot be sure of having grasped an author whole until one has asked and answered (if only to oneself) certain questions about him, even though they may seem to have little to do with the kind of thing he wrote. What were his religious opinions? How did he respond to natural scenery? What was his attitude toward women? toward money? Was he rich or poor? What was his daily routine, his activities on a typical day? etc. Finally, what was his vice or weakness?—for every man has one. Not a single one of these questions is irrelevant in evaluating the author of a book or the book itself, unless it is a treatise on pure geometry, above all if it is a literary work, that is, something in which everything may have a place.

Very often a writer assumes in his writings a posture directly opposed to his own vice or secret bias, in order to dissimulate or hide it, but it remains a detectable and recognizable impression, even though indirect and masked. In anything it is all too easy to adopt the contrary attitude, merely by turning one's fault inside out. Nothing resembles a hollow so much as a protuberance.

What is more common than a public profession of every noble, generous, elevated, disinterested, Christian, philanthropic sentiment? Must I therefore take at face value, and praise for their magnanimity (as I see done daily), the swan's quills or specious tongues that pour out these high-sounding moral marvels? I listen to them unmoved. A certain chill of ostentation puts me off; their words convey no impression of sincerity. I am ready to grant them

18. Karl Viktor von Bonstetten (1745–1832) resembles Voltaire both in his cosmopolitan literary convictions and in the liberalism of his philosophical and confessional writings. Jean François Ducis (1733–1816) made adaptations of Shakespeare's tragedies to suit French dramatic taste.

# On the Literary Tradition

*Like "What Is a Classic?" the following essay, originally delivered in 1857 as the opening lecture of Sainte-Beuve's course in literary history at the Ecole normale, indicates the catholicity of his literary taste. At the same time, it makes explicit the norms, grounded in literary history itself—in the "tradition"—which provide a reasonably objective basis for his final judgments of individual authors and works.*

\* \* \* Who can deny that there is a tradition? It exists clearly marked out for us like one of those huge, broad highways that once crossed the Empire and terminated in the City of Cities. As descendants of the Romans, or at least adopted children of the Latin race which itself was initiated into the cult of Beauty by the Greeks, we must embrace, absorb into our consciousness, and never abandon the heritage of those masters, of that illustrious ancestry, a heritage which from Homer down to the latest classic of yesterday (if such there be)[1] constitutes our intellectual wealth in its purest and most substantial form. This tradition is not made up only of the collection of memorable works which we enshrine in our libraries and pore over. In large measure it informs our laws, institutions, manners, and customs, our unconscious and hereditary education, the very roots of our being. It consists of a certain principle of reason and culture which over the years has gradually colored and modified the very character of this Gallic nation, saturating even the temper of our minds. All this it is our business to preserve from loss and guard from distortion, ready to sound the alarm—should such a thing threaten—as though in the face of a common danger.

What I am about to lay down is not a comparison between two

1. And why not? for us this latest classic was Chateaubriand. [Sainte-Beuve]

14

profoundly distinct and completely unequal orders, but rather a
reconciliation of them that will throw my thought into sharper
relief.

M. de Chateaubriand, thinking of some particularly fine chapters
of the *Esprit des lois*, closed his *Génie du christianisme* by posing this
question: "What would be the state of society today if Christianity
had never appeared on earth?" As may easily be imagined, answers
sprang from everywhere to flow from his pen.

A learned English author, Colonel Mure, in his *History of Greek
Literature*,[2] raises another question: "If the Greek nation had never
existed, or if its works of genius had been annihilated by the grandeur
of the Roman predominance, would the principal modern races of
Europe have attained to any greater height on the ladder of literary
culture than that attained by the other ancient peoples before
Hellenic influence reached them?" This is one of those large,
fascinating questions that more than any others stimulate our
thinking and imagination.

It is one that I myself have very often pondered, gentlemen.
Framing the question in every possible way—taking a number of
examples and looking at it from every viewpoint—I have wondered
what modern literature (to consider nothing else) would have come
to if the Battle of Marathon had been lost and Greece conquered,
crushed, and enslaved before the Periclean Age, even supposing she
had preserved something of the full matchless beauty of her first
great Ionian poets—but without the focusing lens of Athens, where
all light converged.

Let us never forget that Rome, by her energy and skill, had already achieved the widest political power and great national
maturity by the end of the second Punic War, without yet possessing
anything worthy of being called a literature. To become caught up,
through her generals and great men, by the splendid light that was
to double and perpetuate her glory, Rome had to conquer Greece.
Leaving out of account the first Hellenic race so privileged above all
others and so uniquely endowed, how many peoples are or have
been in this respect more or less like the Romans! I mean nations

2. William Mure (1799–1866), *A Critical History of the Language and Literature of
Ancient Greece*, 5 vols. (London, 1854–57).

advent of Alexander: "In thought and eloquence our City has left other men so far behind her that her pupils have become the teachers of others, and she has done so well that the name *Greek* no longer seems to be the designation of a race but of intelligence itself, and men are called Greeks who share our culture rather than our birth." Pericles said the same thing with greater authority in that admirable panegyric on Athens that forms the magnificent heart of his Funeral Eulogy to the warriors who died for their country. No one has ever spoken better of that blessed City, where no gloom or envy, no rigid austerity, offended the sight or mortified the joy of a neighbor; where it was a pleasure simply to live and breathe its air and walk its streets; where the beauty of the architecture, of the bright daylight, and a certain festive atmosphere were alone sufficient to drive away all sadness from the spirit; that city where men loved Beauty combined with simplicity, and philosophy without effeminacy, where wealth was fittingly used and unostentatious, where courage was not blind (like that of the fiery Mars) but enlightened and aware of its reasons (as becomes the city of Minerva). This is the true Athens of Pericles' ideal, his creation and masterwork, the school of Greece (Ἑλλάδος Ἑλλὰς Ἀθηναι) [Athens, the Greece of Greece.] * * *

But the Athenians were able to realize only half his wish, and the great work Pericles dreamed of—and not only dreamed of but actually proposed—a work of perseverance, lasting energy, and universal political dominion, it was the task of the Romans to fulfill on another and much larger scale, no longer by sea but on land. And just when the fallen Greeks, deprived of the exercise of public virtues, were with rare exceptions becoming more frivolous, glib, sophistical, ingratiating, and extravagant than ever before, their conquerors caught hold of the precious divine element, a particle of that Promethean fire, and with it enlivened their practical vigor and solid good sense in a constitution that united ardor with stability. * * * Thus arose the other Supreme City, in the radiance of which Cicero wished that men might live forever and thus be assured against rusting away, the Rome of Catullus and Horace, down to that of the younger Pliny. These are our spiritual homelands.

When, after the reign of the Emperor Trajan, Roman decadence definitely set in, the sacred literature just then coming into being did not inherit literary beauty so quickly or so directly as Rome had done at its first contact with Greece; the torch was not passed on from hand to hand. * * * But when centuries had passed, after revolutions and laboriously completed cultural cycles, the stars come once again into favoring conjunction. Harmony and supreme beauty are rediscovered, to blaze out resplendently in the world of art in that amiable Rome of Raphael under Pope Leo X. In an order less brilliant but perhaps more admirable, the order of morals and eloquent speech, of sincere and earnest poetry, it reappears in France during the reign of Louis XIV. There was a period in which biblical grandeur and Hellenic beauty came together to be fused and mingled in spirit and form into a lofty simplicity. And when today we speak of the tradition and of what would be lacking if it had never been, of what would be missing from the most delectable treasures and noblest frescoes of human memory, we have a right to exclaim on grounds equally incontestable: "Why, there would have been no Homer and Xenophon! There would have been no Virgil! There would have been no *Athalie!*"

But there arose great literary men entirely outside of this tradition. Shall I name them? I know only one such, a very great one indeed, Shakespeare. But are we quite sure that he *is* entirely outside of the tradition? Had he not read Montaigne and Plutarch, those copious repositories, or rather hives, in which so much of the honey of antiquity is stored up? An admirable poet and beyond doubt the most natural since Homer, although in a very different way, a poet of whom it has been written that his imagination is so creative and he paints so well and with such bold energy all characters, from heroes and kings down to tavern keepers and peasants, that "if human nature were destroyed, and no monument left of it except his works, other beings might know *what man was* from these writings."[4] Oh, you gentlemen do not have to be told that this man, so

4. George, Lord Lyttelton, *Dialogues of the Dead.* See *Shakespeare Criticism: A Selection, 1623–1840,* ed. D. Nichol Smith (London: Oxford University Press, 1961), p. 73.

curiosity, Goethe could lose himself in the infinite, the indeterminate. Where would he go if, among the many summits he knew, Olympus no longer took his fancy? Where would he not go, he the most open-minded of men, who ventured farther toward the East than any other? His transformations, his pilgrimages in pursuit of varying forms of the beautiful, would henceforth have no end. But he checks himself, comes to a halt; he knows the vantage point from which the contemplated universe appears in its fairest light. And whenever we wish to form an idea of the critical spirit at its highest degree of intelligence and thoughtful understanding, we picture Goethe, the attentive and vigilant spectator, observant from afar, on the watch for every new discovery and event, for every passing sail on the horizon, but always taking his sight from the heights of a Sunium.[9]

It is he, the author of *Werther* and *Faust*, who uttered—out of personal knowledge—that most fitting aphorism: "I call the classical the healthy and the romantic the sickly." Since the classical, and the romantic too, form parts of the tradition considered in every stage of its development through time, I must pause over this sentence of Goethe's and try to explain it to myself here in your presence.

In its most general character and broadest definition, the classical really comprehends literatures at their moment of health and auspicious bloom, in full accord and harmony with their period, their social matrix, and with the principles and leading powers of society, literatures at peace with themselves; that is to say, content to belong to their nation and time, and to the social order which gives them birth and growth (joy of spirit is said to characterize their strength, which is as true of a literature as of a person); literatures which are and feel themselves to be at home, in their proper medium, not socially outcast or subversive, not having as their basic element malaise, which has never been a basic element of beauty. Far be it from me, gentlemen, to cry down romantic literature; I am sticking to the terms of Goethe and of historical analysis. There is no choosing the moment of one's birth; nor is there any escaping, least of all in childhood, the prevailing winds of one's

9. A promontory in Attica.

time, which may blow dry or damp, bringing fever or health; souls
are subject to such currents. That feeling of immediate contentment,
in which above all there is hope with never a touch of discourage-
ment, in which one has the sense of being at the threshold of an era
stronger and more lasting than oneself, an era that fosters and gives
judgment; of having a goodly field for one's course, for an honorable
and glorious progress in broad sunlight—this feeling provides the
foundation upon which are subsequently erected the regular palaces
and classical temples, works well proportioned. When one lives in
constant public instability and sees society change several times
before one's eyes, one is disinclined to believe in literary im-
mortality and as a result inclined to allow oneself every license. But
no one can provide himself with that confident sense of a stable and
lasting season; it is breathed in with the atmosphere in youthful
hours. Romantic literatures, which are before all else daring and
adventurous, have their merits, their achievements, their brilliant
roles, but outside of the established cultural framework. In two or
three epochs they enjoy their great moment but are never at home
in a single one; they are always uneasy, searching, temperamentally
eccentric, either far in the van or far behind, longing to be elsewhere
—vagrant.

Classical literature never complains or moans, is never "bored."
Anguish sometimes produces or makes possible a greater effect, but
beauty is more tranquil.

The classical, I repeat, numbers among its traits a love of its own
time and place, unaware of any others finer or more desirable; it is
justly proud of them. "Activity in tranquillity" would be its motto.
This is true of the ages of Pericles and Augustus, as it is of the
reign of Louis XIV. Let us listen to them speaking beneath their
fair skies, their azure dome, so to speak—the great poets and
orators of those days. Their hymns of praise still ring in our ears;
their applause was boundless.

The romantic suffers from nostalgia, like Hamlet. It seeks for
what it does not have, even beyond the clouds; it muses, and lives
in dreams. In the nineteenth century it adores the Middle Ages; in
the eighteenth, with Rousseau, it is revolutionary ahead of its time.
In Goethe's sense of the term there are romantics in various periods:

somewhat uncertain stock taking, may well one day renew and perhaps freshen the surface of literary history (though I suspect that literature may have less to gain from it than history!). If that great destroyer Time effaces the memory of many a fact, and annihilates, along with their supporting evidence, valid explications, it is also in many respects the great discoverer; it brings other kinds of evidence suddenly to light and turns up unexpected secrets. Still, this much granted, and not forgetting the constant possibility of further discoveries, let us conserve, if we can, the sensitivity of good taste, with its subtle and immediate receptivity. In the presence of living productions of the human mind, let us dare to keep our critical judgment clear and lively too, keep it sharply defined, unconstrained, and self-confident even without supporting evidence.

I do not hesitate to cite various examples and comparisons, choosing those which will best allow you to share my thought. As you know, over a period of twenty years Thucydides compiled notes for the composition of his austerely beautiful *History*. He must have kept a kind of memoir or detailed journal of all the events he witnessed from the security of his exile. Once he set to work, as an artistic historian he made free use of this material, choosing or rejecting whatever did or did not suit his design, and then either destroyed his notes or gave them no further thought. I do not say that it would not be extremely interesting to have those notes today, had they by some chance been preserved. What I do say is that in the system which would tend to prevail and already does prevail, people would come definitely to prefer them to the composition itself, to that *History of the Peloponnesian War* that is so perfect in form, so epic or dramatic, so rigorous in its unity of action. They would come on the whole to prefer the materials to the finished work, the scaffolding to the monument—Thucydides' notebooks in place of Thucydides' statue of bronze! You who betake yourselves to Athens, who visit there daily, will do your best to resist this inversion of viewpoints, even in what belongs to modern times; and if nowadays truth at any price (or what is taken for truth), or mere inquisitiveness, finally gains ascendancy over art, you will see to it that the ancient method and what emerged from it continue to be honored as objects of worship and study, ever present to the memories and reflections of those faithful intellects still responsive to the idea of beauty.

From this confessed and mutually stipulated inclination to retain —even while taking full advantage of the sometimes rather unwieldy tools of the new criticism—some of the practices and even the principles of the old, giving first place in our admiration and esteem to inventiveness, to composition, to the art of writing, to grace of intellect, to elevation or refinement of talent—from this inclination you will not conclude, gentlemen, that as regards famous books and writers we shall register a monotonous and universal eulogy. The best way not only of responding to fine literary works but of leading others to appreciate them is to have formed no prior judgment, to have a totally receptive attitude each time we read or discuss them; to forget, if possible, that they have been with us a long time, and take them up again as though we had not known them before today. Reinvigorated in this way at their source, our judgments, even if they should sometimes remain inferior to some we have previously come upon, at least regain vitality and freshness. A man of taste, though he may not plan to teach and is completely at leisure, should for his own benefit—I should say every four or five years—review his finest and most settled admirations, subject them to testing and verification as though they were new; in other words, restore them to full consciousness and freshness, even at the risk of seeing them here and there become unsettled, because all that matters is that they be alive. But have no fear for the result. Unless the reader himself has in the meantime become unconsciously less worthy of admiring the beautiful, all or almost all of those previously well founded admirations will gain from this candid review. Things which are truly beautiful appear increasingly so as one grows older and has made more comparisons.

We shall therefore endeavor, gentlemen, not to admire more than we should or otherwise than we should; not to exalt one age, however magnificent, over all others, nor all at once to ascribe every excellence to a few great writers. When we speak of them, we shall try to direct our praise to the principal excellence of each, for even in the great authors there is one principal excellence. Only contemporary writers may possess every kind of excellence, even

# Madame de Sévigné's *Letters*

*This youthful* Portrait *of Madame de Sévigné and the much later* Lundi
on Lord Chesterfield *exemplify Sainte-Beuve's enduring interest in the
literature and personalities of the* ancien régime. *Throughout the neo-
classical age the epistolary art was so consciously cultivated that the personal
letter achieved the status of a minor genre. With his special flair for the
humbler forms of literary expression, Sainte-Beuve found in these two
consummate practitioners congenial subjects.*

The critics, especially the foreign critics, who have most rigorously
judged our two literary ages agree on what constituted the prevailing
characteristic which, reflected in countless ways, accounts for their
greatest splendor and embellishment: a spirit of conversation and
social intercourse; a refined and lively understanding of the seemly
and the ridiculous; an ingenious delicacy of sentiment; a grace,
pungency, and consummate civility of expression. And—with exceptions that will occur to each reader and the mental reservation
of two or three names like Bossuet and Montesquieu—down to about
1789 these qualities indeed formed the distinctive and salient
character of French literature among the other literatures of
Europe. This glory, which has been considered almost a reproach
against our nation, is sufficiently fruitful and beautiful for those who
know how to understand and interpret it.

At the beginning of the seventeenth century, our civilization and
consequently our language and literature still lacked maturity and
self-confidence. As the religious disturbances died down, amid the
intervals of the Thirty Years' War Europe was painfully giving
birth to a new political order; inside France, the last phases of the
civil disorders were wearing to an end. At the court, a few salons,
*ruelles* of wits, were already fashionable; but they were not yet

producing anything great and original, and subsisted on a steady diet of Spanish novels and Italian sonnets and pastorals. Only after Richelieu and the Fronde, under the Queen-mother and Mazarin, in the milieu of the banquets at St. Mandé and de Vaux, the salons at the Hotel de Rambouillet,[1] or the antechambers of the young king, did there suddenly emerge, as though miraculously, three splendid spirits, three geniuses diversely endowed, but all three gifted with a pure and unaffected taste, a perfect simplicity, and a happy copiousness nourished by the graces of an inborn refinement, and destined to initiate a glorious age in which no one else surpassed them. Molière, La Fontaine, and Madame de Sévigné belong to a literary generation which preceded that headed by Racine and Boileau, and they are distinguished from these latter by several traits referable at once to the quality of their genius and the moment of their appearance. It is apparent that by both cast of mind and situation they are closer to the France that existed before Louis XIV, to the older French language and spirit. By their education and their reading they were far more involved in that France of an earlier time, and if foreigners appreciate them less than they do certain later writers, that is owing precisely to what we French find most intimate and most indefinably delightful in their accent and manner. Therefore if today, with good reason, there is a tendency to question and revise many of the judgments pronounced some twenty years ago by the professors at the Atheneum,[2] if relentless war has been declared against many overrated reputations, we can hardly too much uphold and venerate those immortal writers who were the first to bring originality into French literature and endow it with the unique physiognomy it still retains among all literatures.

1. The Fronde was a civil war lasting from 1648 to 1652 aimed at the over-throw of Cardinal Mazarin, who ruled France during Louis XIV's minority.

St. Mandé and Vaux were chateaux belonging to Nicolas Fouquet, finance minister under Louis XIV and literary patron, who spent his final years in prison on a charge of embezzlement. In the earlier seventeenth century a group of aristocratic literati, many of them women, gathered at the salons presided over by Madame de Rambouillet. The studied elegance and ornateness of their manners and speech are brilliantly satirized in Molière's *Les Précieuses ridicules*.

2. Founded in 1803 in Paris, the Atheneum was an establishment for free higher education where Sainte-Beuve attended lectures during his student days.

young nobility upon whom, as the price of his favor, Louis XIV imposes politeness and elegance; and without doubt, beneath that brilliant surface and carousel gilding there are vices enough to overflow once again in another Regency period, especially after they shall have been brought to a state of fermentation by the bigotry of the final years of the preceding reign. But at least the decencies are observed, and opinion has begun to stigmatize everything ignoble and vulgar. Moreover, at the moment when disorderliness and brutality suffered loss through scandal, decency and elegance gained through simplicity. The label of *précieuse* had gone out of fashion; people still recalled, with a smile, having been adherents of that movement, but they were so no longer. * * *

For us, in the year 1829, habituated as we are to practical occupations, it is difficult to form a clear idea of that life of leisure and social converse. Nowadays the world moves so quickly, with so many things coming one after the other upon the scene, that all our waking moments hardly suffice to take them all in. Our daylight hours are passed in study, our evenings in serious discussion; amiable talk, true conversation, is nonexistent. In our time, wherever aristocratic society has most fully preserved the leisurely habits of the last two centuries, it seems to have been able to do so only on condition of remaining a stranger to modern thought and manners. During the period of which we are speaking, that mode of living, far from being a hindrance to keeping abreast of contemporary literature, religion, and politics, was then the best way of doing so; provided you now and then glanced around, out of the corner of your eye, from wherever you were sitting, you could devote the rest of your time to your personal inclinations and your friends. Besides, conversation was not yet what it was to become in the eighteenth century in the salons opened under the presidency of Fontenelle,[4] an occupation, a formal affair, a pretension. One did not necessarily aim at it. Nor was the ostentatious display of geometry, philosophy, and fashionable sentimentality then a requirement; people merely chatted about themselves or others, about little or

4. Bernard Le Bovier de Fontenelle (1657–1757), whose broad interests ranged from poetry to science, argued the superiority of modern over ancient culture in his *Digression sur les anciens et les modernes.*

nothing. As Madame de Sévigné says, there were *endless* conversations: "After dinner," she somewhere writes to her daughter, "we went off to chat in the loveliest woods in the world; there we spent six hours in several kinds of conversation so favorable, tender, friendly, and obliging toward both you and me that I am moved by them."

In the midst of this social activity that was so relaxed and simple, so capricious and gracefully animated, a visit or the receipt of a letter, of no intrinsic importance, were events in which one took pleasure and which one hastened to communicate. From their style and form the most insignificant things took on value. Nonchalantly and without noticing it people made an art even of life itself. Consider Madame de Chaulnes's visit to *Les Rochers*. It has often been said that Madame de Sévigné took great pains with her letters, mindful while writing them if not of posterity at least of her contemporaries, whose approbation she was courting. That is not true; the days of Voiture and Balzac[5] were already long past. Her usual practice was to write offhand, on as many topics as she could, and if time pressed she hardly took the trouble to read over what she had written. "The fact is," she writes, "friends writing to each other should always let their pens run on as they will; mine always jogs along with loose reins." But there were days when she had more leisure or felt more in the mood, and on those occasions, quite naturally, she would take almost the same care in arranging and composing a letter as would La Fontaine one of his fables: for example the letter to M. de Coulanges on her daughter's marriage, or the one about the poor Picard who was discharged for refusing to "toss hay." Letters like these, brilliant for their formal artistry, containing few petty secrets and slanders, caused a stir in the social world and everyone wished to read them. "I mustn't forget to tell you what happened to me this morning," Madame de Coulanges wrote to her friend. " 'Madame,' I was informed, 'one of Madame de Thianges' lackeys is here.' I ordered him to be admitted and this is what he had to say: 'Madame, Madame de Thianges entreats you to send her Madame de Sévigné's letter about the horse, and also

5. Vincent Voiture (1598–1648) and Jean-Louis Guez de Balzac (1594–1654) both wrote highly polished epistolary prose.

frivolous or light-minded because we often see her in a gay and giddy mood. She was serious, even melancholy, especially during her rustic sojourns, and reverie made up a great part of her waking hours. Only, we must be careful not to misconceive this: she did not wander musing along those somber, thick-set, tree-lined avenues, in the vogue of Delphine or Oswald's beloved.[10] That sort of reverie had not yet been invented, and had to wait until 1793, when Madame de Staël would write her admirable *Influence des passions sur le bonheur*. Until then, to muse was an easier, simpler, more personal thing, indulged without self-consciousness. It was thinking of her daugher down in Provence, of her son at Candy or in the king's army, of friends far away or dead. It was writing, as in a letter of August, 1675:

> You know the manner of my life: it is taken up with five or six friends whose company gives me pleasure, and with the thousand duties I am obliged to perform, and it is no small matter. But what vexes me is that these days slip by in doing nothing; our paltry life is made up of such days; we grow old, and we die. I find this very bad.

The strict and regular religion which governed living at that time did much to moderate that libertinism of sensibility and imagination which has since known no restraint. Madame de Sévigné was scrupulously mistrustful of any thoughts that were "ticklish"; it was her express desire that morality be Christian, and she more than once chides her daughter for her infatuation with Cartesianism. She herself bowed her head before the vicissitudes of this life, taking refuge in a sort of providential fatalism inspired by her links with Port-Royal and her reading of Nicole[11] and Saint Augustine. This quality of religious resignation increased in her as she grew older without in any way altering the serenity of her temperament; it often lends to her expression a touch of firmer good sense and graver tenderness. Most notably, there is a letter to M. de Coulanges on the death of the minister Louvois, in which she rises to the sublime of

10. Madame de Staël (1766–1817), best known for her *De l'Allemagne*, wrote the romantic novels *Delphine* and *Corinne*. Oswald is a character in the latter.

11. Pierre Nicole (1625–95) was a Jansenist moralist and theologian at Port-Royal.

Bossuet, as in other, earlier passages she had reached the comic of Molière.

In his estimable studies on Madame de Sévigné, M. de Saint-Surin[12] omitted no occasion of comparing her with Madame de Staël, always to the disadvantage of that celebrated woman. I agree that the comparison is both interesting and rewarding but it ought not to be to the disadvantage of either of them. Madame de Staël represents an entire new society, Madame de Sévigné a society now vanished, whence arise remarkable differences which one might at first be inclined to ascribe to the contrasting casts of mind and temperaments of the two women. Nevertheless, without denying the profound original divergence of these two souls, one of whom knew only maternal love while the other experienced every passion including the noblest and most virile, a closer inspection reveals many shortcomings and virtues common to both, the discrepant developments of which are referable only to the diversity of their times. What light and graceful simplicity, what dazzling pages of pure spirit there are in Madame de Staël, whenever her sentiment is not thwarted and she forgets for a moment her politics and philosophy! And what of Madame de Sévigné—does she never take a moment to philosophize and expound ideas? If not, of what use her ordinary practice of reading Nicole's *Essais de morale*, Balzac's *Socrate chrétien*, and Saint Augustine?—because this woman, so often regarded as frivolous, read everything and read well. Not to enjoy serious literature, she said, "pales the colors" of the mind. She read Rabelais and [Bossuet's] *Histoire des variations, Cléopatre*[13] and Quintilian, Saint John Chrysostom and Tacitus, as well as Virgil not *travestied*[14] *but in all the majesty of the Latin and Italian*. In the rainy season she read several huge folios *in twelve days*. During Lent, it was her delight to lose herself in Bourdaloue's works.[15] From her conduct toward Fouquet when he was in trouble we may infer what self-sacrifice she would have been capable of in time of revolution. If

12. Pierre Tiffon de Saint-Surin published an edition (1810–19) of de Sévigné's *Letters*.

13. A historical romance by Gautier de La Calprenède (ca. 1610–63).

14. The reference is to the burlesque *Virgile travesti* by Paul Scarron (1610–60).

15. Louis Bourdaloue (1632–1704) was an eloquent Jesuit preacher.

she displays a touch of vanity and self-esteem when the king dances with her one evening or pays her a compliment after a production of Racine's *Esther* at Saint-Cyr, would any other of her sex have shown more "philosophy" in her place? Is not Madame de Staël herself said to have gone out of her way to extort a word and glance from the conqueror of Egypt and Italy?[16]  * * *

Madame de Sévigné's style has been so often and so brilliantly evaluated, analyzed, and admired that it is no longer easy to think of a eulogy at once novel and suitable to apply to her; nor do I feel at all disposed to rejuvenate the critical commonplaces by quibbles. I shall content myself with the single general observation that the magnificent writing styles that graced the age of Louis XIV can be linked to two quite different methods, two contrasting manners. In our literature Malherbe[17] and Balzac founded the learned, polished, refined, labored style, which results from moving from conception to expression slowly and by degrees, groping through revisions and erasures. This is the style which Boileau recommended for every occasion; he would have a writer bring his work twenty times back to the loom, polishing and repolishing it again and again. He boasted of having taught Racine how to write easy lines with difficulty. Indeed, Racine is the most perfect model of this style in poetry; Fléchier[18] was less successful at it in prose. But alongside this manner of writing, always rather uniform and academic, there is another, contrastingly free, capricious, and variable, with no traditional method, readily adaptable to every kind of talent and temperament. Montaigne and Régnier had already provided admirable examples of this style, as had Queen Marguerite[19] in her charming memoirs, the work of several "after-dinner" sessions. It is the broad, loose, overflowing style, better adapted to the train of one's thoughts, a "first thing that comes to mind" style, or *prime-sautier* [spontaneous] style, to borrow Montaigne's own expression.

16. Napoleon.

17. François de Malherbe (1555–1628) was a minor lyric poet who effected reforms in French poetic diction and versification.

18. Esprit Fléchier (1632–1710) was Bishop of Nîmes and a writer of memoirs.

19. Mathurin Régnier (1573–1613) composed free-verse imitations of the Roman satirical poets. Marguerite de France (1552–1615) was the wife of King Henry of Navarre.

This is the style employed by La Fontaine and Molière, by Fénelon, Saint-Simon,[20] and Madame de Sévigné. The last-mentioned excels in it. She lets her pen "jog along with loose reins," profusely scattering colors, comparisons, and images, her wit and sensibility flashing out everywhere. And in this way, without willing or suspecting it, she took her place in the first rank of writers in our language. * * *

And now, if in the foregoing I strike some fastidious souls as having gone rather far in my admiration of Madame de Sévigné, let them indulge me a question: Have you read her? And by *read* I do not mean a random perusal of a selection of the letters or a fond dwelling on the two or three that enjoy classic status, * * * I mean making one's way step by step through the whole ten volumes, * * * skipping nothing, "unwinding" it all, as she would say. In short, I mean doing for her as one does for *Clarissa Harlowe*, when one has two free weeks in the country during a spell of rainy weather. After making this far from unpleasant test, let them protest, if they still have heart to do so, against my admiration, assuming they have not forgotten all about it.

*Portraits de femmes*, pp. 3–21 (May, 1829).

20. Louis, duc de Saint-Simon (1675–1755), author of the *Souvenirs*.

# Pascal's Pensées

*This culminating chapter of* Pascal, *the third book of* Port-Royal, *has been ranked by T. S. Eliot "among the most brilliant pages of criticism that Sainte-Beuve ever wrote." The great seventeenth-century Christian moralist exerted a lifelong formative influence on Sainte-Beuve's thinking. Sainte-Beuve recurs to him constantly, apart from two entire essays on the* Pensées *in* Portraits contemporains *and* Causeries du lundi, *written in 1844 and 1852, respectively. Blaise Pascal has in fact been an attractive subject to several critics. The student of English literature may profitably compare Sainte-Beuve's treatment of the* Pensées *with essays on the same subject by Eliot and Walter Pater.*

\* \* \* In the two- or three-hour conversation whose main points are recorded in the prefaces of Etienne Périer and M. de La Chaise,[1] Pascal has left us a quite accurate outline of what he planned to do in the *Pensées*. My aim is to recapture this conversation and bring it back to life, something that can be done, after a fashion, if good use is made of the many "thoughts" which are still Pascal's vibrant speech, and if they are put into the coherent order we can glimpse in the general plan. The result of this procedure will be a complete and luminous summary, not a reconstruction by guesswork but a fairly close restoration of what was actually said.

Pascal's problem is to lead a man, a living soul, to the Christian faith. So one day he is solicited by his friends to reveal the grand design of his contemplated work, details of which he has mentioned

1. Pascal's nephew, Périer, provided a preface for the first edition of the *Pensées* (1670). Jean Filleau de la Chaise was one of the committee, including Pascal's Port-Royal friends Antoine Arnauld and Pierre Nicole, who "edited" the famous posthumous work from the author's undigested fragments. De la Chaise's preface appeared in later printings.

to several persons, but with too little revelation of its overall shape. This must have been around 1658. His plan was already matured yet at the same time still in that state of novelty that makes it delightful to expatiate upon, as the ardor of discovery lends freshness to one's utterance. Who were these friends before whom Pascal gave his explanation and where did the conference take place? The over-discreet prefaces are very careful to avoid telling us, but we may be sure that the elite of Port-Royal were present and that the gathering place was perhaps none other than Port-Royal at Paris. * * *

Pascal begins. First he tells them what he thinks of the customarily invoked proofs of God's existence, the metaphysical and geometric proofs, as well as those derived from the contemplation of nature's works. Without ruling them out, he thinks them immaterial and ineffective, not really adapted to the human heart:

> I shall not here undertake to prove from natural reasons either the existence of God, or the Trinity, or the immortality of the soul, or anything of that kind; not only because I feel it beyond my powers to find anything in nature capable of convincing hardened atheists, but also because that knowledge is useless and barren without Jesus Christ. Were a man persuaded that the numerical proportions were truths incorporeal, eternal, and dependent on a First Truth in which they subsist, called *God*, I should not find that he had made much progress toward salvation.

Of these metaphysical proofs he says that not everyone is impressed by them, and that with the very few who are, the impression lasts only during the time of demonstration. An hour later they are not sure what to think about it and are afraid of having been deceived, with the result that the demonstration has endlessly to be repeated.

He shows that the proofs which best sink into the minds and hearts of men, and determine their behavior, are mainly moral and historical proofs which appeal to certain natural sentiments or to everyday experience. Through these channels are acquired those truths which everyone recognizes as the most indubitable: for example, that there is a city called Rome, that Mohamet existed, that there was a fire of London, and so forth. Only a madman would doubt such truths or hesitate to stake his life on them even for the slightest gain. In the ordinary course of things one can do no better than to rely on these common pathways to certitude. It is therefore upon simple proofs like these, purely moral and historical, proofs no less convincing than the other kind, and more accessible, more penetrating, more up-to-date and ready to hand, that he intends to ground his entire argument.

Such is the general import of Pascal's prolegomena, in which he clearly shuns that method of logical and geometric demonstration, so dear to Arnauld, no less than that unrestricted rationalism which had recently been instituted by Descartes. This latter point is worth special attention.

Descartes takes his stand in systematic skepticism. By a process of philosophic abstraction he divests himself of all his knowledge, habits, and beliefs. He reduces his thinking to thought alone, with the aim of deriving from *that*, and that alone, all it can yield him.

Pascal's whole procedure and enterprise are tantamount to a protest against this radically independent and purely theoretical rationalism. Generally speaking, he makes very little mention of Descartes, but Descartes was much on his mind. He said of him, as everyone knows: "I cannot forgive Descartes; he would have liked to dispense with God in his entire philosophy but he cannot avoid having him provide a flick of His finger to set the world in motion; after that, he has no further use for God." What he here says of Descartes's physics he was also to declare, with some modification in terms, of his metaphysics. He was to find himself unable to "forgive" Descartes that Reason, thus enthroned in naked isolation, which was in addition to everything else an impossibility. Pascal apparently foresaw what was to result from this, including, in the very next generation, those twins of such variant complexion but of mutual support, Malebranche and Spinoza.[2] He himself postulated no exclusively mental being, no abstract metaphysical man. He wants to stick to the real man, to what he was himself and what we all are. On this living man, then, by the rules of a sublime common

2. The thought of these two philosophers may be regarded as extensions of Descartes's system. But whereas Malebranche sought to reconcile the Cartesian dualism of mind and matter with Catholic theology, Spinoza embraced a pantheistic conception of the Deity.

sense guided above all by the impressions of an extraordinary moral sensitivity, he sets himself to reasoning.

Pascal does not split man into parts, locating his reason here, his senses there, his will somewhere else. He does not strive to establish a unique mode of operation for any one of these faculties. He addresses himself to the reason but without prejudice to the rest: "The heart," he well knows, "has its reasons, which the reason knows nothing of; one is aware of countless instances. . . . it is the heart, and not the reason, that is conscious of God. That is what constitutes faith: God felt in the heart." And again:

> The heart has one order, the intellect another, one subject to principles and demonstrations. The heart's order is different. . . . Jesus Christ and Saint Paul have the order of charity, not intellect, for they wished not to teach but to kindle. It was the same with Saint Augustine. This order consists mainly in digressing upon every point that relates to the end, in order to keep it constantly in view.

In like manner, all Pascal's observations are directed toward the "end," the vital, practical conclusion. He addresses himself to the reason, well aware that to touch the heart belongs to someone other than man. But he tries to open that human reason and so direct it that the light from above that must enter the heart need only find its way through this well-prepared opening: an opening of which, to be sure, the divine light has no need if it would be irresistible, but of which it gladly takes advantage if it discovers it, and which oftentimes it awaits.

> Those to whom God has given religion by the sentiment of the heart are richly blessed and most legitimately persuaded; but to those who lack this gift we can give it only by logical argument, while waiting for God to bestow it by the sentiment of the heart, failing which faith is only human, and useless for salvation.—What a difference there is between knowing God and loving Him!

It is in these terms, then, and upon these principles, not by the arduous and risky method of metaphysical certitude but in the language of common moral belief, that Pascal broaches his task. I will try to recapture and trace his line of thought, following the order of the conversation that has been preserved.

Approaching the subject of man, he lays hold of him as he is, *e medio* [in the midst of things], suppressing not a single trait. And he gives a description of him, a painting in which nothing is forgotten that can make known his every aspect, from the furthest horizon that forms his setting to the most secret places of his sordid heart. What an exordium! What a truly and magnificently philosophical Genesis!

> When man looks at himself the first thing he notices is his body, that is, a certain amount of matter that belongs to him. But to understand what this is, it must be compared with everything above it and everything beneath it, in order to recognize its true boundaries.
>
> Therefore let man survey the whole of Nature in the full extent of its majesty; let him take his eyes from the lowly objects about him and gaze upon that brilliant luminary set like an eternal lamp to light the universe; let him see the earth as a mere point compared with the vast orbit described by that star; and let him marvel that this vast orbit itself is but a tiny point measured against those circled by the stars that revolve in the firmament. But if our vision stops there, let our imagination pass beyond; it will sooner grow weary of conceiving than Nature of providing material. This whole visible world is but an imperceptible detail in the ample bosom of Nature. No idea can come near it. In vain do we swell our conceptions beyond imaginable space: we beget mere atoms in comparison to the reality of things. . . .

And all that follows: "Let man, turning back to himself, consider what he is in comparison with all that exists," and so forth.

Thus for the first strokes of his pencil—nature in its magnificence, its illumination, its amplitude, its boundlessness!—the whole encompassed by man, himself a puny being, having as it were *strayed into this sequestered corner of creation.* Yet he is noble too, suspended as he is between the two infinities of greatness and littleness, a mere nothing with respect to the one, a universe with respect to the other. Such is he first presented to us, precariously poised on his frail ladder rung by the hand of Pascal. Nonetheless, it is grandeur that predominates in this initial sketch, because that *feeblest reed in nature,* being a *reed that thinks,* redeems the whole. Even as he considered man in his fallen state Pascal could not help noticing at the very first glance the traces of his former worth. Milton's Adam, at his first appearance, is not provided with a more glorious setting. There are some splendid vestiges of Moses in Pascal's man, and something of the accent of the Eternal answering Job out of the whirlwind. But as Pascal continues his discourse, all this initial grandeur of regal bearing is soon to fall into debasement and ruin.

Note well, however, as Pascal's distinctive mark, this sense of grandeur, this instinct which exalts even at the moment when he aims to humiliate and bring low. In Montaigne there is never such contour, no such majesty of outline; even the passages of his most sustained eloquence are suddenly defiled.

And so this entire first part of the work, or rather (as we prefer to call it) the conversation, of Pascal treats of man considered in his grandeur and vileness, his pride and his vanity, his corruption through self-love, his illusions induced by fancy or habit, and the sudden leaps or upward soarings which redeem him however low he may fall. It treats him, in short, as the complete and continual contradiction that he is, to the point where "he realizes that he is an inscrutable monster"—the final outcry which the demonstrator wrests from the sufferer thus subjected to his piercing scrutiny. We have this first part of the discourse fully represented in the *Pensées*. It constitutes a first act. Let us follow Pascal in some detail, keeping to the natural order in which the "action" of his drama unfolds.

After that magnificent opening portrayal of man fixed and lost like a mere point in the awesome immensity of a universe to which he is nevertheless superior because he can think; having acknowledged that power of thought which soars aloft to be repulsed and frustrated by some obstacle at every instant, that ardent longing somewhere to discover a firm foundation upon which to build a tower that shall rise to the infinite (*but the whole substructure crumbles, and the earth opens to the bottomless gulf*); having thus shaken as though at random this *thinking reed*, and watched him adrift in the flux of objects, Pascal takes up man as he is in himself, to give him moving proof that his ego is the natural root of his every act, a root corrupt.

Just now, in that first vision of man given at the opening of the discourse, even though it is of fallen man, what struck us in Pascal were the remnants of the Mosaic lightning, reminiscences of the Everlasting speaking to Job, reflections of an ancient splendor that might have graced Solomon. Here, as he explores man's inner secrets and probes his transformations and various pretenses, his *ego*, it is none other than La Rochefoucauld whom he brings to mind,[3] whom he equals in the trenchant precision of his analysis and surpasses in the profound magnanimity of his aim and impulse. In Pascal, all those thoughts which reveal and inject with visible dye, as it were, the tiniest hidden veins of human vanity, are not, as with La Rochefoucauld, on the level of merely curious and detached description; they are not offered simply as "proverbs of witty men." In Pascal the details of observation are sustained by a mighty current of thought.

Pascal knew all that La Rochefoucauld knew. * * * He needed only to grasp the main trunk [of man's passions and poses] to be convinced that just as the roots were corrupt so were all the branches.

> Human life is but a perpetual fallacy made up of nothing but mutual deceit and flattery. No one speaks of us when we are present as he does when we are absent. The bond that exists among men is based solely on this mutual delusion; and few friendships would survive if each man knew what his friend says about him when he is not present, although that friend speaks of him sincerely and objectively.
>
> All men naturally hate one another. Everything possible has been done to make concupiscence serve the general welfare, but this is only a dodge, a false image of charity. For at bottom it is nothing but hatred. . . . This sordid foundation of man, this *figmentum malum* [evil image] is only covered over, not removed.

Except for the word *concupiscence*, which implies Christianity, could these thoughts not be La Rochefoucauld's as well as Pascal's?

But Pascal's difference from La Rochefoucauld appears when he observes that since vanity consists in love of self alone—despite the fact that we cannot avoid seeing ourselves to be full of faults and vices and not at all lovable—the "most unjust and criminal passion" is thereby produced, namely, a mortal hatred of that Truth which

3. La Rochefoucauld, whose *Maximes* first appeared in 1665, had not read the *Pensées*, which did not appear until four years later; and Pascal, dead by 1662, did not know the *Maximes*. These two great authors remain entirely original in their similarities. The attempt to establish some sort of communicative link between them in the person of Madame de Sablé rests on pure supposition. [Sainte-Beuve]

condemns us. At this point Pascal cuts short the infinite variety of
pointed and startling deductions in which La Rochefoucauld
delights. La Rochefoucauld, who gladly dwells in the regions of
human vanity and more or less makes a point of cruising in those
latitudes, declares that "they contain many territories yet unex-
plored." He is engaged in a study that has no end.

Pascal is in a hurry and urges us along; for he has peered into the
farthest reaches of the interior, made the entire tour, and in that
winding archipelago a few Cyclades more or less mean little to him if
the whole is one sea of shipwreck and disaster, a sea of grief which
can at any moment cut off one's return to the true homeland by an
impassable barrier. Pascal is in torment; and it is this torment
which forms the motive force of his drama and attaches him to
mankind. Where the other moralists he encounters tarry and enjoy
themselves as though in the land of the lotus-eaters, forgetting the
true homeland, he becomes restless and pushes on. He will not allow
his man to fall asleep, but keeps the goad still pressed against his
bosom, even as he himself feels its sting. So great is this torment that
later on, even though he will have found the way, he will once
again become anxious; only this time he will be hearing a secret
voice in his heart, calming him, and he will repeat to others these
tender words of the Holy Spirit: "Thou wouldst not seek me if thou
didst not possess me; therefore be thou not anxious!" How different
from this was the earlier anxiety!

So now, having explored vanity, he senses on the one hand how
completely "all those inclinations so alien to justice and reason have
their natural root in the human heart," while on the other hand he
recognizes that "whosoever does not detest this vanity in himself,
along with that instinct which induces him to set himself above
everything, is indeed blind, since nothing is so contrary to justice and
truth." It is therefore necessary to hate that which is the natural
root, in other words to hate the thing that loves itself. For, "if there
is a God," he exclaims, "only He must be loved, and not created
beings." Here arises a new contradiction: how escape it? In this
first section of his discourse, Pascal delights in raising contradictions
on every hand, in besieging man with them, in squeezing him
between alternatives to the point of arousing agony. By this process

he checkmates and subdues him, with the aim of leading him to mercy at the feet of the Truth.

So far his game is hardly begun; he is to carry it further. In all that bears on *the weakness of man, the uncertainty of his natural knowledge with respect to justice and truth, the delusions of his sense and his reason,* on all these points Pascal falls in with and for a considerable way accompanies Montaigne and Hobbes, just as he came within hailing distance of La Rochefoucauld.

With respect to Montaigne, it most often seems as though Pascal's thoughts in these passages were no more than notes taken from memory after reading Montaigne, notes always enhanced and invigorated by some bright touch of his own. Pascal's note taking is not the note taking of an ordinary person.

Now a subtle change of tone becomes perceptible. At this stage of his exposition Pascal remits the repeated intrusions of his own anguish and passion for truth that were apparent when he was dealing directly with human vanity. When he comes to examine man struggling with custom, he seems content to let him go his own way, to watch him stumble along as the noble youths of Sparta used to watch the drunken Helots reel in public without restraining them. There is a lofty irony in the tranquillity Pascal displays throughout this chapter.

Anyone listening to this part of Pascal's discourse would have been struck by its peculiar tone, and by the strange, silent ridicule suddenly visible in the countenance of this penitent soul: "My friend, you were born on this side of the mountain; it is therefore just that your elder brother inherit everything."—"Why are you going to kill me?" "Why not? Don't you live on the other side of the water . . . ?" * * * Finding men everywhere in borrowed character and slaves to the whimsies of custom, he must have been tempted to jolt them with some of Molière's bitterest laughter: "Man is so constituted that he believes himself to be a blockhead merely by being told so; and he makes himself believe it by repeating it to himself."

Hearing Pascal on the subject of *power* and the ascendancy of *fact*, one is appalled by the clarity of his determination. "The laws of the land are the only universal rules in ordinary matters, and in all else

the will of the majority. How so? because they have the power."
"Concupiscence and power are the sources of all our actions:
concupiscence, of our voluntary actions; power, of our involuntary
actions."

By *concupiscence*, understand *egotistical desire*, and you have the
doctrine of Hobbes and of greater men than he, of the most powerful
men who have ever exercised control over their fellows.[4] * * *
However, as we listen to Pascal letting himself go on this theme and
so emphatically denying the existence of natural law, I can imagine
the ingenuous Arnauld, somewhat taken aback, almost interrupting
him, had he not been restrained by the movement, the commanding
tone, and the dazzling brilliance of these lordly pronouncements.

The rare constancy of Pascal's insight is perhaps nowhere more
manifest than when he turns to the social order; here there is
nothing abstract in his thinking. He had seen the Fronde and
studied it closely, being at that time in the man-of-the-world phase
of his life. He had meditated on Cromwell. This early experience
gave him an understanding of whatever directs the enquiring spirit
(once aroused) to questions about states and the origins of society,
an understanding extending far beyond the political science of his
day. "Accustomed to contemplate the prodigies of man's imagination" and of human delusion, he knew how much "pomp and
reverence" a mere hundred years can confer on accepted customs;
he also knew how easily, in the bosom of fickle mankind, ancient
institutions can be overturned by a moment of free and penetrating
scrutiny.

> The art of rebelling and overthrowing states consists in unsettling
> established customs, in probing their origins with a view to pointing
> out their lack of justice. "We must," men say, "revert to the basic
> primitive laws of the state, which unjust customs have annulled."
> This is an unfailing device for destroying everything: *weighed in that*

4. One day Frederick the Great said to Sulzer, who was speaking of the goodness of human nature: "Don't you believe it; you philosophical gentlemen cannot
be acquainted with it. But believe one who has followed the profession of king for
over thirty years: tis a wicked race, with very few exceptions; they must be kept
down." In 1806 Napoleon wrote to his brother Joseph: "Men are base, creeping
things, submissive to force only." [Sainte-Beuve]

*scale nothing will be legitimate.* Nonetheless, the people readily lend ear
to this kind of talk. They shake off the yoke as soon as they take it to be
such, and the socially powerful gain at the cost of ruining both the
people and those prying examiners of received customs. . . .

In these words, and in others in their immediate context, we have
Pascal's political theory, which corresponds to that of Machiavelli
taken in its best sense, the political theory that is most devoid of
commonplaces. There is no reason to be surprised that Pascal in his
time, like Montaigne in his, was a royalist, and that he was so
precisely out of a concern for the peoples' welfare and a contempt
for the depraved ambition of the powerful few. But he goes further
than Montaigne. He lays his finger unhesitatingly, and with a boldness given to very few thinkers at any time, on the very basis of the
social order, as this basis has been constituted for centuries from the
very beginning, a constitution which nowadays we pride ourselves
on having completely turned upside down. Today the intention is
to remake all institutions according to reason. Pascal reveals the
preexisting reality which subsequently makes shift to represent
itself in the guise of right, and which, once so represented, becomes
properly worthy of respect. The reason he gives for sometimes
preferring the will of the majority is, he tells us, "because it is
visible and has the power to make itself obeyed; nevertheless, *it is
the opinion of the least qualified.*"

Moreover, all of a sudden, as though afraid of having gone too
far in his disdain of mankind and having too severely affronted the
great mass of the human race by placing them at the mercy of mere
social custom, he makes them a kind of reparation by giving the
reason for some popular beliefs and setting the peoples' wisdom
against that of the self-styled experts. For Pascal is before all else
human, even in his irony; * * * Therein lies the essential quality
of this "sublime misanthrope," as Voltaire calls him. * * *

At moments, Pascal breaks the orderly procedure of his discourse
and appears to be deliberately incoherent, in this respect acting as
he says nature acts in its movements, the ebb and flow of the sea for
example. "It recedes and returns, then recedes farther, then half as
far, then farther than ever." Thus there are comings and goings,
approaches, respites, and renewals—in short, climaxes calculated, on

every issue, to unseat a human judgment and force a crisis to its utmost. In this first part we have the key to his procedure.

Without dwelling longer on this point, we need only perceive that, having for some moments dealt soothingly with man, Pascal, as though impatient, once again takes rough hold of him, puts him back on the rack, and puts himself there with him. For with Pascal the man he so bitterly assails is himself, just as the man for whom he suffers such agonies of personal anxiety is all mankind. It has been well said that in Pascal the pronoun "I" stands, by a sort of proxy, for the human race; that part of his consciousness most directed toward his own salvation concurs and becomes one with the most universal charity. Once again then, Pascal begins to recapitulate the wretchedness of man and (as though he had not already done so) to set in mutual collision his perpetual boredom, his dread of repose, his insane heedlessness, his vain and tumultuous flight from himself. All this becomes a single-voiced lamentation, inexhaustible and agonizing, a succession of strophes or verses ranging in manner all the way from the Book of Job to Byron. In fact, since it was said that "man that is born of woman is of few days, and full of trouble"; since one man, speaking for all, cried out, "Let the day perish wherein I was born, and the night in which it was said, There is a man child conceived!" since "my calamity laid in the balances" was "found heavier than the sands of the sea," and "the terrors of God do set themselves in array against me"—since those days what has been written more lugubrious and mournful than the following (and so many other similar passages)?

> Imagine a number of men in chains, all condemned to death, some of them each day being butchered in the sight of the others; those who remain see their own condition in that of their fellows, and looking at each other in anguish and helplessness, await their turn: there you have an image of the human condition.

Having reached this lowest point of distress, Pascal recovers himself and once again takes up the contrary theme, gathering together the scattered vestiges of man's grandeur. The prisoner rattles his chains. A light has broken through. The love of truth in his heart does not appear to him to have been annihilated by the hatred of truth, which is also in his heart. "Let man therefore rate himself at his true value," he exclaims; "let him cherish himself, for he has within himself a nature capable of good." But how can this good, this enlightened affection, be attained by man himself alone? Hardly has he caught a glimpse of that chance gleam through the bars of his prison, when he relapses:

*Quaesivit coelo lucem, ingemuitque reperta.*[5]

We are spectators to all the vicissitudes of this drama of the Christian Prometheus, the first act of which closes with this outcry that has rung in our ears from the outset:

What a fantastic being then is man? what a heap of inconsistencies, what an unnatural creature! Judge of all things, imbecile earthworm, depository of truth, cesspool of uncertainty and error, glory and scum of the universe! Who can unravel this enigma? . . . If he boasts, I humble him; if he humbles himself, I laud him; I continue to contradict him until he understands that he is an incomprehensible monster.[6]

This entire section of Pascal's work, in which he takes man to task and convinces him of his nullity, inconsistency, and eternal fluctuation, is entirely adequate as we have it; there is scarcely any fault to be found in it. It would have made little difference if the verses of the Book of Job had been pronounced in one order rather than another. I do not know who said that the fragments of Archilochus[7] are like "broken javelins that still whistle in their flight." The same can be said of Pascal's fragments.

5. "She [Dido] sought for the light in the skies and then groaned when it was found." Virgil *Aeneid* 4, line 692.

6. Compare Alexander Pope:

> Chaos of thought and passion, all confused;
> Still by himself abused, or disabused;
> Created half to rise, and half to fall;
> Great lord of all things, yet a prey to all;
> Sole judge of truth, in endless error hurled:
> The glory, jest, and riddle of the world!
> *An Essay on Man*, 2, lines 13–18.

7. A seventh-century Greek lyric poet whose work survives only in eloquent fragments.

Man thus persuaded, and alerted to his true state, it remains to lead him to Christianity; but we have not arrived there yet. We must make our way step by step. The bond by which Pascal holds man, and which he never again slackens, is infinite anxiety, "the impossibility of being unconcerned" (the exact opposite of Montaigne's pillow[8]): by this bond he draws him. And at this point come new prolegomena, forming a sort of prologue to the next act.

What Pascal could least forgive was that strange repose in some men which he took to be the ultimate sign of *stupidity*. And so by every possible means he prods at this slumber of the mind; he insults it and would render it impossible.

> The immortality of the soul is a matter which is so very important to us and affects us so profoundly, that one must have become entirely senseless to be indifferent about understanding it. . . . I can feel only pity for those who suffer in a state of sincere doubt about it . . . ; but as to those who pass their lives without thinking of that final end of life . . . , this negligence in a matter in which they themselves are at stake, their eternal lives, their very all, incenses me more than it moves me to pity; it astounds and horrifies me; I find it simply monstrous.—It is monstrous to see in the same heart and at the same moment this sensitive concern for the slightest things along with this strange insensibility toward the very greatest things.—It is an incomprehensible bewitchment, a supernatural drowsiness. . . .—Nonetheless, it is entirely certain that man is so perverted that there is implanted in his heart a seed of joy in this. . . .

And he reverts to his image of the prisoner in his dungeon who has only an hour to learn whether sentence has been passed on him, time enough, if he puts it to good use, for getting the sentence revoked. "It is against nature that he should employ that hour not in making enquiries but in playing cards."

Pascal numbered such "card players" among his acquaintances, respectable people, amiable Epicurean types who affirmed quite simply that "nature wishes us to enjoy life all we can and to die

8. Sainte-Beuve's reference is apparently to a sentence in Montaigne's essay "Of Experience": "Oh, what a soft, gentle, and healthful pillow, on which to repose a well-formed head, are ignorance and indifference!"

without thinking about it." Without the slightest doubt he had known some who, like Saint-Evremond, found the death of Petronius to be by comparison "the finest in all antiquity"; for if Socrates died as a truly wise man, "with indifference enough," he nonetheless sought to assure himself as to his status in the next life, discussed the question endlessly with his followers, and, in a word, "for him his death was something worth thinking about"—whereas "Petronius alone faced his with indolence and nonchalance."[9] It was this light-hearted nonchalance that angered Pascal and prompted him to observe: "Nothing is more shameful than to act with bravado before God." To those who boasted of their skill at quick calculation and gambling odds, he spoke their own language; he countered with the rule of necessary *choice* (not of *wagers*), a kind of proof which nowadays we find somewhat shocking when applied to religion and which was thoroughly discussed and perhaps refuted by the eighteenth-century geometers. Be that as it may, it takes no great geometer to see that, given a single awesome chance against an infinity of other possibilities, if we thought long about it, it would loom large enough to determine our actions "just in case." What keeps away fear is thoughtlessness; what tranquilizes is universal diversion. But Pascal soon turned back to those more exalted and more impressive moral arguments, and in those he abounded. The sacred fire flowed from his lips. In this vein he appears to us dazzling and splendid in his wrath, splendid with the flaming beauty of the angel who harries the fainthearted Adam, the sword pressed against his back, and forces him to go forth out of Eden.

Thus Pascal has goaded man and sent him in quest of salvation, a quest outside himself, since within there is only nullity, abyss, contradiction, indecipherable enigma. Whither will he direct himself, this man who seeks? To whom shall he appeal? First to the philosophers, on whose banner the word "Truth" is inscribed in capitals. There follows a full recital of the various philosophies. And now Pascal does what Montaigne did in his *Apologie de Raimond*

9. Saint-Evremond, *Jugement sur Pétrone*. [Sainte-Beuve]
Charles de Saint-Evremond (1610–1703) was a French critic and dramatist. When Petronius, Nero's friend and fellow voluptuary, supposed author of the *Satyricon*, was accused of treason, he ended his life by calmly opening his veins.

*Sebond*, taking up the philosophers singly and in pairs, pitting them against each other and tumbling them head over heels.

> Thus there is open war among men, in which each must choose sides and of necessity align himself with either Dogmatism or Skepticism; for whoever chooses to remain neutral will thereby be a complete Skeptic. That neutrality is the essence of the skeptical sect. . . . What will become of you, oh Man, who seek to know your true condition through your natural reason? . . . You can neither escape one of these sects nor subsist in either of them.

Since in these philosophies that promise so much man has discovered outside himself only the same inconsistency he has already recognized within himself, what in fact is to become of him? For here he is, by this perpetual exaltation and abasement thrown back upon himself, dizzier, more bewildered and dazzled, in short, "a monster who recognizes that he is more inscrutable" than ever. Only after he has deliberately reduced him to this condition, weary, harassed, pitiful, does Pascal begin to point his finger at what may well be the one salvation, Religion. For at last Religion arises and, without yet revealing her name, in spirit speaks these words:

> In vain, oh men, do you seek the remedy for your sufferings within yourselves. All your wisdom can end only in the recognition that within yourselves you shall find neither truth nor well-being. The philosophers have promised you these, but they have failed. They understood neither your true welfare nor your true condition. How could they have supplied remedies for your troubles when they did not so much as understand them? Your chief ills are the pride which separates you from God, the concupiscence which binds you to the earth; their efforts have done no less than nourish one of these ills. If they recommended God as the ideal it was only to exercise your vainglory; they encouraged you to think your own nature equal and consistent with His. And those who saw the vanity of this pretension have cast you into the other abyss, by giving you to understand that your nature was on a level with that of the beasts, and induced you to seek your happiness in lusts, which is the lot of the animals.—This is not the method by which you can be cured of your wrongs, which those sages have not at all understood. I alone can make you see what you are. . . .

These are indeed the words of Religion. But of *which* religion? At the sound of this voice, whose accent gives him new life, man renews his survey of the universe to discover which is the true religion, as he has already done with the philosophies. In fact, would not the God of whom all speak be more likely to have left some tangible evidence of Himself in the sanctuaries than in the schools?—Here there naturally follows an enumeration of the chief known religions, the Mohammedan, the ancient Greek and Roman, the Egyptian, the Chinese.—None of these religions satisfies Pascal's man any more than he was just now satisfied by the philosophies. Their morality, which he mainly examines, shocks or disgusts him, for after all he already knows that a worthy religion must unite and conciliate men. "The true faith would have to inculcate grandeur and wretchedness, to conduce to both self-esteem and self-contempt, to love and to hatred." Instead of this, the swarm of religions that he surveys all appear to expand and exaggerate, even more than the philosophies dared to do, certain isolated elements of man's make-up, while disregarding or suppressing others. And in most cases this tendency gave rise to the most frightful monstrosities and to practices completely criminal. He is gripped by horror. Where then is the place of refuge? did he not have to resign himself to death?

Not until he has arrived at this pass, once again not knowing where to turn, does he catch a glimpse of a particular people in a tiny corner of the world, separated from the other peoples and possessing one of the oldest histories. The discovery of this people astonishes him and attracts him for their very many singular and marvelous characteristics; he never leaves them again.

This people is governed by a single book, which comprises at once their history, their law, their religion. As soon as suffering man has opened this book, he learns that the world is the creation of a God; that this God has created man in His image and implanted in him a likeness of His sovereign grandeur. This first idea pleases suffering man and strikes him as a reliable explanation of certain signs and hints of greatness which he feels in himself, but not of the contrary vileness subsisting along with it. Continuing to read, however, he discovers that man, created in a state of innocence and beauty, transgressed through his own free choice and was hurled into the most justly deserved of calamities. This new state seems to him to correspond exactly to that interior contradiction of which he was so persuaded, and which he has hitherto found so unaccountable.

*A man weary of seeking God through his intellect alone, who begins to read Holy Scripture*—this image forms the second magnificent overture to Pascal's plan, the second Genesis, the one which leads directly to life.

Pascal has his sorrowing man, now just beginning to descry a ray of hope, survey still other passages of this book.

He points out to him that man is no longer spoken of there except in relation to this state of weakness and disorder; that it is often said there that all flesh is corrupt, that men are abandoned to their senses, and that they have a propensity to evil from the moment of their birth. He then shows him how that first fall is the source not only of what is most incomprehensible in man's nature, but also of an infinite number of consequences which are outside himself, the cause of which he does not know. In short, he shows him man so well portrayed throughout this book, that *he appears not different from that first description of him* that he sketched out earlier.[10]

This is excellent. Here is the wheel come full circle, the moral link of the Holy Book joined with the moral link of that other book, the human heart. Unfortunately, we do not have Pascal's whole moral exegesis of the Old Testament. But much as we should like to hear from his mouth the moral teachings of Moses, David, and Solomon, with the elusive added ingredient of the sweeter voice of a Joseph, we can easily supplement what is lacking to the gist of it. His nephew Etienne Périer has furnished us an accurate account of the steps in his explication.

Pascal does not fail to point out what is immediately apparent from the very first page of Holy Scripture: that along with a full understanding of suffering man there is the remedy for his sufferings and *the means of consolation.* Moreover, he finds it wonderful that this book is the only one which speaks worthily of the Supreme Being, the only one that grounds the essence of His worship in the *love* of the God who is worshiped. These are the first features that leap to view when we open the book.

10. Etienne Périer's preface to the *Pensées*. [Sainte-Beuve]

To this point, Pascal has yet to enter upon his chapter on the direct and positive proofs of God's existence, but he has, if one may say so, done more: he has put him whom he is directing into a frame of mind conducive to receiving them with delight, and desiring them. This has amounted to a preparation made on his behalf, a kind of moral pressure, a thorough reduction to submission, or (to put it plainly) a piously skillful contrivance for beating him down in favor of the faith, which henceforth appears venerable and attractive.

Above all, attractive.—Religion has not yet been proven before it has been already insinuated and almost "sanctified" by a morality so divine and so conformable to this human heart.

Moreover, even in the sketchy and imperfect state in which Pascal's plan remains, we can perceive all his skill and superior management. His procedure has been so adroit that from this moment and for the rest of the demonstration the man whom he is leading by the hand, as it were, has been imbued with an inward wish to believe, and is in danger of complicity with his guide.

Nevertheless, Pascal does turn to the evidence in the chapter entitled "The Jews Considered as Trustees of the True Religion" and in the chapters following. Dwelling in particular on the Book of Moses, and using every argument which the criticism of his time could provide, he affirms that it is as impossible that Moses would have left false scriptures behind him as that the people to whom he left them were liable to have been deceived. He speaks of the great miracles reported in this book, and maintains that they cannot be false, as much because of the already established authority of the book as because of all the circumstances that accompany them. * * * He comes at last to the greatest of the proofs of Jesus Christ, namely the Prophecies; and by a host of special insights which he has on this subject he carries it even to the point of making us see the evidence for thinking this to be the one proof among them all for which God has made fullest provision.—It is on this subject of the Prophecies that in the conversation mentioned above Pascal surpassed himself, and those listening to him so attentively were *as though enraptured*.

And in fact, sensual though we have become, by reading these mystic fragments of Pascal's we can easily imagine the effect that this abundance of new explications—some ingenious, some sublime— must have produced on an audience already persuaded—all those bold pronouncements so often repeated since, but striking on the occasion of their first utterance:

When the word of God, which is genuine, is false literally, it is true spiritually. . . .

Everything turns to good for the Chosen, even to the dark passages of Scripture . . . , and everything turns to evil for the others, even to the clear passages. . . .

It is just that so pure a God should reveal Himself only to those whose heart has been purified.

A single saying of David or Moses, such as "You will circumcise men's hearts," enables us to judge of their spirit. . . .

We in turn can find among Pascal's testimonies and arguments a few of those "determinative" traits which he saw in David and Moses, those lightning flashes from the cloudy depths that cancel the dark interspaces. Admittedly, these occur only at instants. The lightning flashes out, and the darkness returns. * * *

After the Old Testament, Pascal turns to the New. He begins with Jesus Christ; and although he has already invincibly proved His existence by the Prophecies and the symbolic language of the Law, of which he sees in Christ the perfect fulfillment, he confirms these proofs by considering His person, both divine and human, the circumstances of His miracles, and the character of His teaching down to the very style of His discourse.

When we have to speak of Jesus Christ, even using the words of Pascal, we feel a kind of involuntary restriction. Unless we pronounce it on our knees in an act of worship, we are afraid of profaning this ineffable name merely by repeating it, a name to which the profoundest reverence may still be blasphemy. * * *

In Pascal, in the part of his discourse [devoted to Jesus Christ], the predominant note is a radiant love. He is caught up and ravished by the mystery of Jesus. What overwhelming love! what affection! what merging of everything in the one Mediator! Taken in its totality, I see this book of the *Pensées*, so clothed in light, outwardly so armed with severity and dread yet at bottom so tender and

mellow, as a sevenfold ark of cedar overlaid with gold and im-
penetrable steel, within which is enshrined—naked, tender, suffering, and joyous—the most bleeding and most sacrificial heart of the
Lamb. Did even Saint John, the Apostle of love, ever have a greater
tenderness and sympathetic sweetness than does this Archimedes[11]
in tears at the foot of the cross? * * *

Charity, Charity before all else, is Pascal's sighing outcry from the
moment he comes to Jesus Christ. At the end of that admirable
passage where in the scale of carnal, intellectual, and spiritual
grandeurs, in connection with the various Orders of veneration and
royalty, Archimedes is so magnificently placed as the Prince of
earthly intellects, there appears Jesus Christ, likewise Prince of His
Order, but of an Order of Holiness, with all the refulgence of that
Order, in His advent in gentleness, humility, and long-suffering, and
for that very reason in great ceremony and preternatural splendor,
visible to the eyes of the heart, eyes that can see Wisdom:

> All bodies, the earth and its kingdoms, do not equal the least of
> minds, for it knows them all, and itself; and bodies know nothing.
> All bodies together, and all minds together, and all they produce,
> do not equal the slightest impulse of Charity. . . .

"Properly understood, all human probity is only a sham imitation
of Charity, and what a wretched copy it is!"[12] As in the Apostle,
this appeal to the one true Charity appears everywhere in the discourse and illuminates it: "The one object of the Scriptures is
Charity. . . ." "Truth without Charity is not God, but an idol. . . ."
This idea resounds throughout, in every key. It is the constant surge
and overflow, the endlessly throbbing and lamenting ebb and flow
of Pascal's thought from the moment he has gained Jesus Christ and
that divine Friend calls to him from Calvary: "I thought of thee in
my agony: I spilled such drops of blood for thee!" We have reached
the goal.

Such, in essence, as nearly as we have been able to grasp it, is the
plan of the great work; or rather such is the discourse as we have

11. A reference to Pascal's discoveries in mathematics and mechanics.
12. Sainte-Beuve's note ascribes this last quotation to La Chaise's preface to the
*Pensées*.

now pieced it together from the very lips of the eloquent Christian. Does it follow that we have nothing to regret, but \* \* \* should rather be glad that the work was never completed and that we can therefore discriminate each *pensée* more thoroughly and more in its particularity? I think this would be going much too far, and now that we have done our best we should confess our deficiency. We know Pascal's purpose, course, and method; but *literarily* (if this word is allowed me and I may use it without disfavor), we have not the slightest notion of what this book of *Pensées* would have been as a product of compositional craftsmanship. Pascal's general style is familiar to us; and from the stylistic point of view alone it is perhaps best that it underwent no reworking. In these hasty notations, in this conversation at once voluble and urgent, we admire audacities of manner which in all likelihood the writer would subsequently have toned down. We are grateful to him for more than one stroke which upon reflection he would perhaps have expunged or softened. In this regard Pascal gains, if anything, by having been intercepted and surprised in the situation of a great unconscious literary artist. But, still and all, how many happy strokes of imagination, how many great and inspired discoveries we have lost! \* \* \*

Moreover, the reputation of [Pascal's] style is established and when once the public takes to admiring, the most diffident are not those who hang back. I will therefore not try to outdo others in praising what is great and simple. The fundamental characteristic of Pascal's style, that solid and unadorned simplicity, has been relished and unanimously described by all good judges from M. de Ribeyran[13] \* \* \* to Fontanes. The latter has very truly observed that Pascal's style cannot be imitated. Given intelligence, one can sometimes put together something in the manner of Montaigne, of Balzac (easily), even a bit of Rousseau or Montesquieu, but not of Pascal or Voltaire. Pascal is more striking than Voltaire, but the prose of neither offers anything of that "trick of how it's done" that lends itself to imitation and counterfeiting. There is only one way to mimic these men, and that is to have their thoughts. \* \* \*

*Port-Royal*, Book III, pp. 418–64 (1848).

13. Otherwise obscure, Ribeyran, archdeacon of Cominges, was one of several readers who praised the *Pensées* at its first appearance.

# Lord Chesterfield's Letters to His Son

*Quite apart from the appeal of his superb epistolary art, Chesterfield was a subject especially engaging to Sainte-Beuve on two other counts. He was a near-perfect embodiment of that moderation, clarity of expression, and urbanity which characterized his cultural period, qualities especially esteemed by Sainte-Beuve, who devoted nearly one hundred of the* Lundis *to eighteenth-century figures. There is the additional appeal of Chesterfield's generous admiration for French letters and manners (though not French politics), a theme that forms a kind of leitmotif in Sainte-Beuve's appraisal.*

In every historical period there have been treatises designed for the education of the proper gentleman, the courtier (when gentlemen lived only for courts), the complete cavalier. In these many treatises on good breeding and refinement, if we open them in later ages, the first thing we notice is social roles as bygone as our ancestors' fashions in dress; the model has since obviously changed. If we look closely, however, and the book is one written by someone of good sense who is acquainted with real men, we may still gain something from the study of the models that were held up to preceding generations. The letters Lord Chesterfield addressed to his son, which contain a whole school of good breeding and worldly knowledge, are of particular interest in that he had no thought of proposing a model, but only of privately educating an excellent pupil. These are confidential letters which were suddenly made public, revealing all the secrets and the ingenious expedients of paternal solicitude. If, reading them today, we are struck by the importance given to accidental and ephemeral particulars, to mere details of dress, we are no less struck by the more durable parts, by what belongs to human observation at any time; and these latter parts are much more considerable than one might gather at first glance. In addressing

64

himself to the son he wished to educate in what becomes the
well-bred man in society, Lord Chesterfield did not produce a
treatise *On Duty*, like Cicero's; but he left letters which, by their
mixture of correctness and lightness of touch, by subtly uniting a
certain flippancy of tone with solid graces, occupy a mid-position
between the *Mémoires du Chevalier de Grammont*[1] and *Télémaque*.

Before speaking of them in some detail, we should know a little
about Lord Chesterfield himself, one of the most brilliant minds of
the England of his time and one of the most intimately connected
with France. Philip Dormer Stanhope, Earl of Chesterfield, was born
in London on September 22, 1694, the same year as Voltaire.
Descendant of an illustrious family, whose worth he appreciated and
whose honor he wished to uphold, he nonetheless found it hard not
to laugh at overdone genealogical pretensions. To insure himself
once for all against this bias, he had two aged figures, male and
female, hung among the portraits of his ancestors. Beneath one was
written "Adam Stanhope" and beneath the other "Eve Stanhope."
In this way, without slighting honor, he put an end to fanciful
whims.

His father had nothing to do with his education; the boy was left
to the care of his grandmother, Lady Halifax. From his earliest
years he felt a desire to excel in everything, the same desire which
later on he would have liked to excite in the heart of his son, and
which for good or ill is the motive of every great enterprise. Since
he himself when very young had received no guidance, he more than
once mistook the objects of his emulation and grasped at false honor.
He confesses that during a period of inexperience he fell into heavy
drinking and other excesses to which otherwise he had no natural
inclination except that it pleased his vanity to hear himself styled a
man of pleasure. It was the same with gambling, which he thought
an indispensable ingredient in the make-up of the fashionable young
man. At first he plunged into it without passion but was subsequently unable to break free, and in this way for a considerable time

1. The reference is to the *Mémoires du comte de Grammont*, notable for their
incisive and witty account of English court life. They were written in 1704 by
Anthony Hamilton at the presumed dictation of his brother-in-law Philibert,
comte de Gramont.

jeopardized his fortune. "Take warning from my behavior," he told his son; "make your own choice of your pleasures and do not let them be imposed upon you."

The desire to stand out and distinguish himself did not always go awry in this manner, for he often applied it properly. His first studies were of the finest kind. Sent to the University of Cambridge, he learned everything they taught there, civil law, philosophy, and the course in mathematics given by the blind scholar Saunderson. He read Greek fluently and sent accounts of his progress, written in French, to his former preceptor, M. Jouneau, a French refugee clergyman. Lord Chesterfield had learned our language during his childhood from a Norman chambermaid of his household. When Chesterfield last visited Paris, in 1741, M. de Fontenelle, noticing a trace of the accent of Normandy in his pronunciation, mentioned this fact and asked him whether he had not first learned our language from someone of that province, which was in fact true.

After two years at the university, he made the Grand Tour of the Continent, following the custom of the young noblemen of his country. He visited Holland, Italy, and France. To that same M. Jouneau he wrote from Paris on December 4, 1714:

> Je ne vous dirai pas mes sentiments des Français, parce que je suis fort souvent pris pour un d'eux, et plus d'un Français m'a fait le plus grand compliment qu'ils croient pouvoir faire à personne, qui est: *Monsieur, vous êtes tout comme nous.* Je vous dirai seulement que je suis insolent, que je parle beaucoup, bien haut et d'un ton de maître; que je chante et que je danse en marchant, et enfin que je fais une dépense furieuse en poudre, plumets, gants blancs, etc.[2]

Here we see the mocking, satiric, and slightly insolent tone in which he starts off with a witticism at our expense; later on he will do justice to our serious qualities.

2. "I will not tell you what I think of the French because I am very often taken for one of them, and more than one Frenchman has paid me what they consider the greatest possible compliment they can pay anyone, which is: 'Sir, you are exactly like us.' I'll only tell you that I am insolent, that I talk a great deal, very loud and authoritatively; that I sing and dance while walking, and finally that I spend a frightful amount on powder, plumes, white gloves, etc."

In the letters to his son, he has pictured himself on the first day of his entrance into good society as still covered with his Cambridge rust—bashful, embarrassed, tongue-tied—finally gathering the courage to say to a pretty lady next to him: "Madame, do you not find it very warm today?" But Lord Chesterfield told his son about this incident only to keep him from being discouraged and to show him how far he himself had had to progress. He cites his own example in order to embolden his son and draw him closer to himself. I should be very wary of taking this anecdote literally. If Lord Chesterfield was ever for a moment embarrassed in society, that moment must have been very brief indeed.

Queen Anne had just died and Chesterfield hailed the advent of the House of Hanover, of which he was to become an avowed champion. At first he had a seat in the House of Commons, where he got off to a good start. A seemingly trifling circumstance, however, is said to have held him back and somewhat paralyzed his eloquence. One of the members of the House, distinguished by no other outstanding talent, had a trick of imitating and counterfeiting to perfection the speakers whom he answered. Chesterfield dreaded ridicule (this was a weakness of his), and on certain occasions remained silent more than he would have liked for fear of exposing himself to the mimicry of his colleague and opponent. Soon, at the death of his father, he inherited the peerage, and moved on to the House of Lords, where the setting was perhaps better suited to the grace, subtlety, and urbanity of his eloquence. Yet he did not consider these two public stages to be comparable in the relative importance of the debates or the political influence to be gained in them. "Such an event, I believe, was never read nor heard of," he later said of Pitt when that great orator agreed to enter the upper chamber under the title of Lord Chatham.

> To withdraw, in the fullness of his power, and in the utmost gratification of his ambition, from the House of Commons, (which procured him his power, and which alone could insure it to him) and to go into that Hospital of Incurables, the House of Lords. . . .

I need not give here an evaluation of Lord Chesterfield's political career. But if I dared hazard a general judgment, I should say that his ambitions were never fully satisfied, and that the shining honors that filled his public existence concealed, deep down, many a disappointed desire and the wasting of many hopes. Twice, on the two crucial occasions of his political life, he failed. While still young and in the first ardor of his ambition, he had early staked his all on the side of the heir presumptive to the throne, who became George II; he was among those who at the advent of that prince (1727) had most reason to count on his favor and a share in power. But this skillful man, though desirous of facing toward the rising sun, failed to orient himself with perfect precision. He had long paid court to the prince's mistress, in the belief that she was to become influential, and he had neglected the legitimate wife, the future queen, who however alone held the real authority. Queen Caroline never forgave him. This, the first setback in Lord Chesterfield's political fortunes, occurred when he was thirty-three and in the full tide of his hopes. In his too eager haste he had taken a false step. Robert Walpole, less clever and outwardly less keen, had arranged and contrived things better.

Thrown conspicuously into the opposition, especially after 1732 when he was obliged to resign his court posts, Lord Chesterfield labored with all his strength at Walpole's fall, which did not occur until 1742. But even then he inherited no power and was not included in the new coalitions. When, two years later, in 1744, he did enter the administration, first as ambassador to The Hague and Lord Lieutenant of Ireland, then even as Secretary of State and a member of the Cabinet (1746–48), it was in a capacity more specious than real. In short, Lord Chesterfield, at all times a considerable political figure in his country, whether as opposition leader or as skilled diplomat, was never a leading minister or even a very influential one.

In politics, he certainly had that far-ranging perception and that vision of the future which make for mental enlargement, but he was doubtless more fully possessed of these virtues than he was of the persevering patience and practical steadiness which are so necessary to men in government. Of him as of La Rochefoucauld it can be truly said that politics served mainly to turn an imperfect man of action into an accomplished moralist.

In 1744, when he was only fifty, his political ambition seemed already partly worn out and his health so far impaired that he thought preferably of retirement. Besides, we now know the object of his secret ideal and true ambition. Around 1732, before his marriage, by a French lady (Mme Du Bouchet) he had met in Holland he had had a natural son, to whom he had become very tenderly attached. To this son he wrote in all sincerity: "From the time that you have had life, it has been the principal and favorite object of mine, to make you as perfect as the imperfections of human nature will allow." It was toward the education of this son that his every wish, his every affectionate and worldly predilection, had been directed, and though Lord Lieutenant in Ireland or Secretary of State in London, he found time to write him long, detailed letters in order to guide him in the slightest contingencies and perfect him in gravity and refinement.

The Chesterfield we most love to study is therefore the man of wit and experience who engaged in worldly affairs and essayed every role of political and public life only to discern the most elusive springs of their operation, and to tell us the last word about them. It is the Chesterfield who from youth was the friend of Pope and Bolingbroke, the introducer to England of Montesquieu and Voltaire, the correspondent of Fontenelle and Madame de Tencin;[3] the Chesterfield whom the Académie des Inscriptions adopted into its membership, who united the spirit of the two nations, and who, in a witty essay, but particularly in the letters to his son, reveals himself to us as a moralist as obliging as he is accomplished—one of the masters of living. It is England's La Rochefoucauld whom we are studying.

After the publication of the *Esprit des lois*, Montesquieu wrote to the Abbé de Guasco, then in England: "Tell my Lord Chesterfield that nothing flatters me so much as his approbation, but that since he has read me three times he will be in all the better position to tell me what has to be corrected and rectified in my work: nothing would be more instructive to me than his observations and criticism." It was Chesterfield who, speaking one day to Montesquieu of the

3. Alexandrine de Tencin (1682–1749) was a patroness of writers and herself the author of the novel *Mémoires du comte de Comminges*.

hastiness of the French for revolutions and their impatience with slow reform, uttered words which sum up our whole history: "You French know how to set up barricades, but you will never erect barriers."

There can be no doubt of Lord Chesterfield's relish for Voltaire. Of the *Siècle de Louis XIV* he observed: "Lord Bolingbroke had just taught me how history should be read; Voltaire shows me how it should be written." But at the same time, with that practical good sense which hardly ever abandons intellectual people on the other side of the English Channel, he sensed Voltaire's indiscretions and disapproved of them. When already old and entirely withdrawn from the world, he wrote to a French lady:

> Vos bons auteurs sont ma principale ressource; Voltaire surtout me charme, à son impiété près, dont il ne peut s'empêcher de larder tout ce qu'il écrit, et qu'il ferait mieux de supprimer sagement, puisqu'au bout du compte on ne doit pas troubler l'ordre établi. Que chacun pense comme il veut, mais qu'il ne communique pas ses idées dès qu'elles sont de nature à pouvoir troubler le repos de la société.[4]

What he wrote here in 1768, Chesterfield had already said over twenty-five years earlier when writing to Crébillon the younger,[5] his special correspondent and confidant in moral matters. Once again it was about Voltaire, the subject being his tragedy *Mahomet* and the rash things in it: "Ce que je ne lui pardonne pas, et qui n'est pas pardonnable," Chesterfield wrote to Crébillon,

> c'est tous les mouvements qu'il se donne pour la propagation d'une doctrine aussi pernicieuse à la société civile que contraire à la religion générale de tous les pays. Je doute fort s'il est permis à un homme d'écrire contre le culte et la croyance de son pays, quand même il serait de bonne foi persuadé qu'il y eût des erreurs, à cause du trouble et du désordre qu'il y pourrait causer; mais je suis bien sûr qu'il n'est

4. "Your fine authors are my principal resort; Voltaire above all delights me, all except his impiety, with which he can't help larding everything he writes and which he would do better wisely to suppress, since in the last analysis one ought not to disturb the established order. Let everyone think as he will, or rather as he can, but not communicate his ideas when they become such as may disturb the repose of society."

5. Son of Crébillon the tragic poet, Claude de Crébillon (1707–77) wrote *Le Sopha* and other comic novels.

nullement permis d'attaquer les fondements de la morale, et de rompre des liens si nécessaires et déjà trop faibles pour retenir les hommes dans le devoir.[6]

In speaking thus, Chesterfield was not mistaken about Voltaire's great inconsistency. This inconsistency, simply put, is that Voltaire, who delighted in regarding men as madmen or children and could never sufficiently laugh them to scorn, at the same time placed loaded weapons in their hands, never troubling himself as to what use they might put them to.

In the view of the Puritans of his own country, it might be said, Lord Chesterfield himself stood accused of having undermined morality in the letters addressed to his son. The austere [Samuel] Johnson, who in other respects was not unbiased toward Chesterfield and thought himself wronged by him, said on the publication of these letters that "they teach the morals of a whore and the manners of a dancing master."[7]

Such a judgment is unjust in the extreme, and if Chesterfield in given instances puts so much stress on graceful manners and the amenities, to the neglect of all else, it is because he has already covered the more substantial aspects of education, and because his pupil is in no danger of falling short in the things which make a man *respectable* but in those which make him *attractive*. Although more than one passage of these letters may seem strange coming from a father to his son, in their entirety they are informed by a spirit of tenderness and sobriety. If Horace had a son, I imagine he would hardly have spoken to him in any other fashion.

The letters begin with the ABCs of education and instruction. Chesterfield explains and sums up in French for his son the rudiments of mythology and history. I do not at all regret that these

6. "What I cannot forgive him, and is not to be forgiven, are his many efforts to propagate a doctrine as pernicious to civil society as it is contrary to the general religion of every country. I very much doubt whether a man is free to write against the divine worship and faith of his country, even if he is sincerely convinced that they are erroneous, because of the disturbance and disorder he might bring about; but I am entirely certain that it is absolutely forbidden to attack the foundations of morality and to break the bonds, so necessary and already so weak, that keep men to their duty."

7. As quoted in Boswell's *Life of Johnson.*

first letters were published; they contain some early bits of excellent advice. Little Stanhope is not yet eight years old when his father draws him up a little rhetoric suited to his capacities, and tries to imbue him with the idea of good speech and elegance in his manner of expressing himself. He especially urges upon him *attention* in all he does, giving the word its full value. It is attention alone, he tells the boy, that impresses things on the memory. "There is no surer sign in the world of a little, weak mind than inattention. Whatever is worth doing at all, is worth doing well, and nothing can be well done without attention." This precept he reiterates constantly, varying its applications as his son grows older and becomes better able to understand their full extent. Whether it is pleasure or study, he wants everything that is done to be done well and only at its proper time, without being distracted by anything else. "When you read Horace attend to the justness of his thoughts, to the happiness of his diction, and the beauty of his poetry, and do not think of Puffendorf, *de Homine et Cive;*[8] and when you are reading Puffendorf, do not think of Madame de Saint-Germain; nor of Puffendorf when you are talking to Madame de Saint-Germain." But this steady and rigorous submission of one's train of thought to the commands of the will is the property of great or of very fine minds only.

M. Royer-Collard[9] used to say "that what our times mostly lacked was *deference* in the moral order and *attentiveness* in the intellectual order." In his less ponderous way, Lord Chesterfield might well have said the same thing. He was not long in sensing what was lacking in the child he wished to educate and whom he made his chief care and purpose in life. "In the strict scrutiny that I have made into you," he told him, "I have (thank God) hitherto not discovered any vice of the heart, or any particular weakness of the head; but I have discovered laziness, inattention, indifference; faults which are only pardonable in old men, who, in the decline of life, when health and spirits fail, have a kind of claim to that sort of tranquillity. But a young man should be ambitious to shine and

8. Chesterfield's reference is apparently to the *De officio hominis et civis* by the German jurist Baron Samuel von Pufendorf (1632–94).

9. Pierre-Paul Royer-Collard (1763–1845) lectured on philosophy at the Sorbonne from 1811 to 1814.

excel." Yet it was precisely this sacred fire, this spark which makes the Achilles, Alexanders, and Caesars "be first in every undertaking," the motto of greathearted and eminent men in every field, that nature had at the outset failed to implant in the honest but fundamentally mediocre soul of young Stanhope. "You seem to want that *vivida vis animi* [lively power of the spirit]," his father told him, "which spurs and excites most young men to please, to shine, to excel." "When I was of your age," he says again, "I should have been ashamed if any boy of that age had learned his book better, or played any game better than I did; and I would not have rested a moment till I had got before him." This whole little course of education by letters offers throughout a kind of dramatic interest. In them we trace the struggle of a refined, elegant, energetic nature, as Lord Chesterfield's was, as it grapples with an upright but indolent disposition, a soft and sluggish clay which it wants at all costs to mold into a finished, attractive masterpiece but which it succeeds after all in making only into a more or less adequate and estimable copy. In this struggle, in which so much art is expended, and the endless advice, under so many metamorphoses, is always essentially the same advice, what holds and even comes close to moving the reader is the genuine paternal affection which animates and inspires the refined and excellent teacher, here as patient as he is acute, marvelous in expedients and skill, never discouraged, inexhaustible in sowing in an ungrateful soil the seeds of elegance and grace. Not that this son, the object of so much zealous cultivation, was in any respect unworthy of his father. It has been claimed that nothing was more lumpish and more sullen than he, and an unfeeling remark of Johnson's to this effect is quoted. This is a caricature that goes beyond the truth. By more accurate testimony it would seem that Mr. Stanhope, though no model of gracefulness, had in fact all the appearance of a well-bred man, refined and decent. But is this not precisely the most disheartening thing about the whole enterprise? It would have been better to have failed entirely and managed only to have formed an original character in the reverse sense, whereas in having succeeded, with so much trouble and expense, only in producing an ordinary and insignificant man of the world, the sort of person of whom one's whole judgment consists in saying that there is nothing to say about him, there was indeed reason for being in despair and pitying one's product, were one anything else than a father.

In order to enliven his son and give him that affability that cannot be acquired later on, Lord Chesterfield had from the very beginning thought of France. From intimate letters written to a Parisian lady, who I believe was Mme de Monconseil, we learn that he had thought of sending him there while he was still a child. "J'ai un garçon," he wrote this lady,

> qui à cette heure a treize ans. Je vous avouerai naturellement qu'il n'est pas légitime; mais sa mère est une personne bien née, et qui a eu des bontés pour moi que je ne méritais pas. Pour le garçon, peut-être est-ce prévention, mais je le trouve aimable; c'est une jolie figure, il a beaucoup de vivacité et, je crois, de l'esprit pour son âge. Il parle français parfaitement, il sait beaucoup de latin et de grec, et il a l'histoire ancienne et moderne au bout des doigts. Il est à présent à l'école; mais comme ici on ne songe pas à former les moeurs ou les manières des jeunes gens, et qu'ils sont presque tous nigauds, gauches et impolis, enfin tels que vous les voyez quand ils viennent à Paris à l'âge de vingt ou vingt-et-un ans, je ne veux pas que mon garçon reste assez ici pour prendre ce mauvais pli; c'est pourquoi, quand il aura quatorze ans, je compte de l'envoyer à Paris. . . . Comme j'aime infiniment cet enfant, et que je me pique d'en faire quelque chose de bon, puisque je crois que l'étoffe y est, mon idée est de réunir en sa personne ce que jusqu'ici je n'ai jamais trouvé en la même personne, je veux dire ce qu'il y a de meilleur dans les deux nations.[10]

10. "I have a son who is just thirteen. Of course I will confess to you that he is not legitimate; but his mother is a person of good family who has been kinder to me than I deserved. As for the boy, perhaps it is prejudice, but I find him likable; he is a pretty figure, he has a great deal of liveliness and, I think, intelligence for his age. He speaks French perfectly, he knows a great deal of Latin and Greek, and he has ancient and modern history at his finger tips. At the moment he is at school; but as no one here ever thinks of training the morals or manners of young men, and they are almost all silly, awkward and rude, in a word, just as you see them when they come to Paris at the age of twenty or twenty-one, I do not wish my boy to remain here and take on these bad habits. This is why I plan to send him to Paris when he becomes fourteen. . . . Since I am exceedingly fond of this child, and pride myself on making something good of him because I think he has the makings, my idea is to unite in him what I have hitherto never found in a single person, I mean the best of both nations."

And he goes into the details of his project and the means he plans to use: an English tutor in the mornings, a French preceptor for after dinner, with the help above all of the *beau monde* and good company. The supervening war between England and France put off this Parisian educational project, and the young man did not make his debut at Paris until 1751, at the age of nineteen, after completing his tours of Switzerland, Germany, and Italy.

Everything was arranged by the most attentive of fathers to assure his success and his welcome on this new stage. The young man is housed in the Academy, with M. de La Guérinière; he does his exercises there in the mornings and is to devote the rest of the day to society. "Pleasure is now the last branch of your education," writes this indulgent father; "it will soften and polish your manners, it will excite you to seek and at length to acquire the *graces*." But on this latter point he proved to be exacting and uncompromising. He harps constantly on the *graces*, because without them all effort is in vain. "If they do not come to you, carry them off," he exclaims. This was an easy thing for him to say: as if, in order to be able to carry them off, one did not need to have them already.

Three ladies among his father's friends are especially charged with overseeing and guiding the young man's debut, his acknowledged "governesses," Mme de Monconseil, Lady Hervey, and Mme Du Bocage. But these initiators seem essential only at the beginning; the young man must subsequently proceed on his own and choose a charming and more intimate guide. On this delicate subject of women, Lord Chesterfield breaks the ice: "I will not address myself to you upon this subject, either in a religious, a moral, or a parental style. I will even lay aside my age, remember yours, and speak to you, as a man of pleasure, if he had parts too, would speak to another." And he expresses himself accordingly, to the best of his ability urging the young man toward "honest arrangements" and delicate pleasures, in order to dissuade him from gross and licentious habits. He accepts the principle "that an honest arrangement is becoming to a gallant man." In this matter his whole morality is epitomized in this verse of Voltaire's:

*Il n'est jamais de mal en bonne compagnie.*[11]

11. "There is never any evil in good company."

It was especially at these passages that the sedate Johnson's modesty hid its face; our own modesty merely smiles at them.

The weighty and the trifling are everywhere mingled in these letters. Marcel, the dancing master, is recommended very often; no less so is Montesquieu. The Abbé de Guasco, a kind of hanger-on of Montesquieu, is a person useful for gaining entrée here and there. "Between you and me," Chesterfield writes, "he has more knowledge than parts. *Mais un habile homme sait tirer parti de tout* [But a clever man knows how to profit by everything]; and everybody is good for something. President Montesquieu is, in every sense, a most useful acquaintance. *He has parts joined to great reading and knowledge of the world. Puisez dans cette source tant que vous pourrez* [Draw all you can from that spring]."

Among authors, those whom Chesterfield chiefly recommends at this period and who most habitually recur in his advice are La Rochefoucauld and La Bruyère. ". . . if you read in the morning some of La Rochefoucauld's maxims, consider them, examine them well, and compare them with the real characters you meet with in the evening. Read La Bruyère in the morning, and see in the evening whether his pictures are like." But these excellent guides ought to have no other use than as geographical maps. Without direct observation and experience they would be useless and would even lead into error as much as a geographical map might do, if someone wished to get from it a complete knowledge of cities and provinces. Better read one man than ten books. "The world is a country which nobody ever yet knew by description: one must travel through it oneself, to be acquainted with it."

Here are some precepts or observations of Chesterfield which are worthy of those masters of human morality he commends:

> The most material knowledge of all, I mean the knowledge of the world, is never to be acquired without great attention; and I know many old people, who, though they have lived long in the world, are but children still as to the knowledge of it, from their levity and inattention.
>
> Human nature is the same all over the world; but its operations are so varied by education and habit, that one must see it in all its dresses in order to be intimately acquainted with it.
>
> Almost all people are born with all the passions, to a certain degree;

but almost every man has a prevailing one, to which the others are subordinate. Search everyone for that ruling passion, pry into the recesses of his heart, and observe the different workings of the same passion in different people. And, when you have found out the prevailing passion of any man, remember never to trust him where that passion is concerned.

If you would particularly gain the affection and friendship of particular people, whether men or women, endeavour to find out their predominant excellency, if they have one, and their prevailing weakness, which everybody has, and do justice to the one and *something more than justice to the other.*

Women have, in general, but one object, which is their beauty, upon which scarcely any flattery is too gross for them to swallow.

Women who are either indisputably beautiful or indisputably ugly are best flattered upon the score of their understandings.

On the subject of women again, if he sometimes seems very disdainful, he makes them reparation elsewhere; least of all, whatever he may think of them, will he permit his son to slander them unduly.

You seem to think that, from Eve downwards, they have done a great deal of mischief. As for *that lady*, I give her up to you; but, since her time, history will inform you that men have done much more mischief in the world than women; and, to say the truth, I would not advise you to trust either more than is absolutely necessary. But this I will advise you to, which is, never to attack whole bodies of any kind.

Individuals forgive sometimes; but bodies and societies never do.

In general, Chesterfield recommends circumspection to his son, and a kind of prudent neutrality, even toward those impostors and fools the world swarms with. "Their enmity is the next dangerous thing to their friendship." This is the morality not of a Cato or a Zeno, but of an Alcibiades, an Aristippus or an Atticus.

In response to some peremptory opinions his son had expressed on the subject of religion, he will say: "Every man's reason is, and must be, his guide; and I may as well expect that every man should be of my size and complexion, as that he should reason just as I do."

In all things he favors knowing and loving the good or the best, but not making himself their champion against all men. Even in literature it is necessary to be tolerant of others' shortcomings: "Leave them in the tranquil enjoyment of their errors in taste as well as in religion." Oh, what a gap separates such wisdom from this harsh trade of criticism as we practice it!

Yet he does not counsel lying; on this point he is explicit. His precept is this: Don't tell everything, but never lie. "I have always observed," he is fond of saying, "that the greatest fools are the greatest liars. For my own part, I judge of every man's truth by his degree of understanding."

Clearly, the serious in him is easily mingled with the agreeable. Always and everywhere he requires of the spirit both the solid and the subtle, gentleness of manner with underlying strength. Lord Chesterfield fully sensed the graver side of France and all that the eighteenth century bore within it that was fertile and formidable. According to him, "Duclos,[12] in his *Reflections*, has very truly observed, *qu'il y a un germe de raison qui commence à se développer en France* [that there is a seed of reason beginning to sprout in France]. But this I foresee," Chesterfield adds, "that before the end of this century, the trade of both king and priest will not be half as good a one as it has been." As early as 1750 our Revolution is clearly predicted in his writings.

From the outset he cautions his son against the notion that the French are frivolous. "The colder northern nations generally look upon France as a whistling, singing, dancing, frivolous nation; this notion is far from being a true one, though many *petits-maîtres* [fops] by their behaviour seem to justify it, but those very *petits-maîtres*, when mellowed by age and experience, very often turn out very able men." The ideal, as he sees it, would be to unite the merits of the two nations; but in this mixture he still seems to lean toward the French side. "I have often said, and do think, that a Frenchman, who, with a fund of virtue, learning, and good sense, has the manners and breeding of his country, is the perfection of human nature."

He himself combines well enough the advantages of both nations,

12. Charles Duclos (1704–72) was a French moralist.

although with a trait very characteristic of his race. He has imagination in his very wit. Hamilton[13] himself has this distinctive trait and
carries it into his French wit. Bacon, the great moralist, is almost a
poet in his expression. Not so much can be said of Lord Chesterfield
and yet he has more imagination in his sallies and witty expressions
than one can find in Saint-Evremond and in our own artful moralists
in general. In this respect he takes after his friend Montesquieu.

If, in the letters to his son, we can without undue severity point
out a few instances of a slightly tainted morality, we should in
compensation indicate some very sober and entirely admirable
passages, in which he speaks of Cardinal de Retz, Mazarin, Bolingbroke, Marlborough,[14] and many others. It is a rich book. Not a
page of it can be read without retaining some happy observation.

Lord Chesterfield had in mind a diplomatic career for this much
beloved son. At first he found some difficulties in the way of his
prospects, for reasons having to do with the boy's illegitimate
birth. To silence any objections, he had his son enter Parliament;
this was the surest way to overcome the scruples of the Court.
During his maiden speech Mr. Stanhope hesitated a moment and
was forced to resort to his notes. He never again underwent the
test of a public address. He seems to have succeeded better in
diplomacy, in those secondary roles in which solid merit alone
suffices. He occupied the post of Envoy Extraordinary at the Court
of Dresden. But his health, always delicate, had declined before its
time, and his father suffered the grief of seeing him die before
himself, scarcely thirty-six years old (1768).

At this period Lord Chesterfield was living entirely sequestered
from the world because of his infirmities, of which the most distressing to him was total deafness. Montesquieu, whose sight was
failing, had once said to him, "I know how to be blind." But it was

13. See note 1 above.
14. Cardinal de Retz (1613–79), prelate and author of a masterly volume of
*Mémoires;* Cardinal Mazarin (1602–61) succeeded Richelieu as de facto ruler of
France; Lord Bolingbroke (1678–1751) was an English statesman and philosopher;
the Duke of Marlborough (1650–1722) led the English army to a series of brilliant
victories over the French during the War of the Spanish Succession.

not like Lord Chesterfield to say as much; he did not know how to be deaf. He said even more than this about it in letters to his friends, even to his French friends. "The exchange of letters," he remarked, "is the conversation of deaf people and the only bond of their society." He found his last consolation in his pretty country house at Blackheath, which he also baptized *à la française* with the name of *Babiole*. There he busied himself with gardening and raising his melons and pineapples. It pleased his fancy to vegetate "along with them."

"J'ai végété toute cette année," he wrote to one of his French female friends in September 1753,

> sans plaisirs et sans peines: mon âge et ma surdité me défendent les premiers; ma philosophie, ou peut-être mon tempérament (car on s'y trompe souvent), me garantit des dernières. Je tire toujours le meilleur parti que je puis des amusements tranquilles du jardinage, de la promenade et de la lecture, moyennant quoi *j'attends la mort, sans la désirer ou la craindre*.[15]

He undertook no lengthy projects, for which he felt too fatigued, but occasionally sent pleasant essays to a periodical publication, *The World*. These essays fully come up to his reputation for refinement and urbanity. Nothing, however, approaches the work which for him was not a "work," the letters which he never intended having anyone read but which today constitute the stock of his literary wealth.

His old age, somewhat premature, was long drawn out. On this sad theme his wit played in a hundred different ways. Of himself and of his friend Lord Tyrawley, equally aged and infirm, he said, "Tyrawley and I have been dead these two years; but we don't choose to have it known."

Voltaire, who though always pretending to be at the point of death had remained more youthful, wrote to him on October 24, 1771, this charming letter, signed "The Sick Old Man of Ferney":

15. "I have vegetated all this year, without pleasures or pains. My advanced age and my deafness deny me the former; my philosophy or perhaps my temperament (for we often confuse the two) insure me against the latter. I get the best I can from the quiet diversions of gardening, going on walks, and reading, by which means I await death without desiring or fearing it."

. . . Enjoy an honorable and happy old age, having gone through the trials of life. Enjoy your wit and preserve your body's health. Of the five senses given us, you have but one that is weakened, and Lord Huntingdon assures me that your stomach is good, which is well worth two ears. I might perhaps be in a position to judge which is sadder, to be deaf or blind, or to be able to digest. I can judge knowingly of these three conditions, but it is a long time since I have dared to judge of trifling matters, let alone of things so important. I am content merely to think that if you have some sunshine in the beautiful house you have built, you will have some bearable moments; that is all that can be hoped for at our age. Cicero wrote a fine treatise on old age, but he did not substantiate his book by the facts: his last years were extremely miserable. You have lived longer and more happily than he. You have had to deal with neither perpetual dictators nor triumvirs. Your prize has been and remains one of the most desirable in that great lottery in which winning tickets are so rare and the grand prize of uninterrupted happiness has never yet been won by anyone. Your philosophy has never yet been disturbed by the vain fancies that have sometimes addled fairly sound brains. *In no respect have you ever been either charlatan or dupe of charlatans*, and this I hold to be a most uncommon merit, which contributes to the shadow of felicity that one can enjoy in this short life.

Lord Chesterfield died on March 24, 1773. In calling attention to his charming course in worldly education, we thought it not unfitting to take lessons in good manners and politeness, even in a democracy, and to receive them from a man whose name is so closely associated with those of Montesquieu and Voltaire; who, more than any of his contemporary countrymen, showed a special partiality for our nation; who relished, perhaps beyond reason, our amiable qualities and was conscious of our solid excellences; and of whom it could be said in full praise that he had a French mind, if he had not revealed even in his zest and in the sprightliness of his wit that indefinable touch of the imaginative and the colorful which stamps him at last with the seal of his race.

*Causeries du lundi*, II, 226–46 (June 24, 1850).

# What Is a Classic?

*Viewed historically, Sainte-Beuve's best-known* Lundi *takes its place in the long and continuing debate over the troublesome terms* classic *and* romantic. *No doubt its popularity, notably among English-speaking readers, owes much to its being read as an eloquent plea for tolerance, for that broad taste to which* classic *is neither a period label nor a term polar to* romantic, *indicative of the second-rate. A true classic, Sainte-Beuve declares, is any author, irrespective of period or style, "who has enriched the human spirit." Yet in the light of his serious reservations about romanticism elsewhere, his tolerance seems curiously restricted. As a plea for catholicity of taste, "What Is a Classic?" itself is ambiguous, both in its quotation of Goethe's characterization of the classic as "healthy" and the romantic as "sickly," and in the noteworthy absence from Sainte-Beuve's visionary Parnassus of a single writer from the Romantic Age. The uncertainty of his position is hardly removed by a footnote to "On the Literary Tradition" which somewhat grudgingly concedes classic status to the romantic Chateaubriand (see above, page 14). Sainte-Beuve's real achievement lies in broadening the term* classic *beyond the narrow and rigidly exclusive concept of French classical theory.*

A delicate question capable of quite different solutions, depending on the period and the moral climate. An intelligent man put it to me just today, and I want to try, if not to solve it, at least to examine and debate it before my readers, if only to induce them to answer it themselves, and to clarify their conception of it as well as my own. After all, why shouldn't one now and then take the risk in criticism of dealing with a few of those subjects which do not concern persons, in which some issue rather than some individual is discussed, and of which our neighbors the English have so well succeeded in constructing an entire genre modestly called Essays? Granted, in order to treat subjects of this kind, which are always a bit abstract and intellectual, it is advisable to speak in tranquillity, to be sure of one's own and of other peoples' attention, and to avail oneself of one of those moments of quiet, moderation, and leisure which are rarely accorded to our amiable France and which her bright genius hardly tolerates even when she is on her good behavior and is no longer making revolutions.

According to the usual definition, a classic is an ancient author already hallowed in admiration and an authority in his genre. The word *classic*, taken in this sense, first appears among the Romans. With them, not all the citizens of the various social classes but only those of the first rank, who possessed an income above a certain figure, were properly called *classici*. All those with a lower income were designated by the phrase *infra classem*, meaning beneath the preeminent class. We find the word *classicus* used by Aulus Gellius[1] in the figurative sense, applied to writers: a writer of value and note, *classicus assiduus que scriptor*, a writer who counts, a writer of substance, discriminated from the proletarian mass. Such an expression implies an age advanced to the extent that there has already been a kind of census and classification in literature.

For the moderns, originally, the true and only classics were naturally the ancients. The Greeks, who by a special good fortune and as a ready relief of spirit had no other classics than themselves, were at first the only classics of the Romans, who took pains and taxed their ingenuity to imitate them. After the glorious periods of their literature, after Cicero and Virgil, the Romans in turn had their own classics, and these became almost exclusively those of the following centuries. The Middle Ages, which were less ignorant of Latin antiquity than one might suppose, but which were lacking in moderation and good taste, confused ranks and orders: Ovid was rated above Homer, and Boethius[2] seemed a classic equal at least to Plato. The literary Renaissance of the fifteenth and sixteenth

1. Aulus Gellius was the second-century Latin author of *Noctes Atticae*, a miscellany of information about the literary, philosophical, historical, and scientific learning of his time.

2. Boethius was a sixth-century Christian Roman philosopher and poet, highly regarded in Medieval times. His chief work is *De consolatione philosophiae*.

centuries clarified this age-old confusion and then only did esteem fall into a proper gradation. From then on, the true classical authors of the two antiquities stood out clearly against a luminous background and grouped themselves harmoniously on their twin hills.

Meanwhile the modern literatures had come into being and the more precocious of them, such as the Italian, already had their own kind of antiquity. Dante had appeared, and his posterity had early hailed him as a classic. Italian poetry may well have declined since then, but it has always regained and kept a certain impetus and echo of that lofty origin whenever it wished to do so. It is no small advantage for a poetry thus to take its point of departure, its classical wellspring, from high eminence, and to descend, for example, from a Dante, rather than to make its way laboriously upward from a Malherbe.

Modern Italy had her classics, and Spain had every right to think that she possessed hers as well, while France was still in quest of hers. The fact is that a few talented writers favored by originality and exceptional zest, a few efforts brilliant but isolated and without consequence, soon interrupted and always to be renewed, do not suffice to endow a nation with this solid and imposing fund of literary wealth. The very idea of the classical implies something that has succession and consistency, that forms a whole and a tradition, something self-creating and self-transmitting, something that endures. Not until after the splendid years of Louis XIV did the nation become aware with a thrill of pride that it had experienced this good fortune. Every voice declared it to Louis XIV with flattery, exaggeration, and pomposity, but still with a certain feeling of truth. At this time there appeared a singular and pointed contradiction: the men most taken with the marvels of the age of Louis *le Grand*, to the point of sacrificing all the ancients to the moderns, those headed by Perrault, tended to exalt and sanctify the very persons whom they encountered as their most ardent opponents and adversaries. Boileau avenged and angrily upheld the ancients against Perrault, who extolled the moderns, namely, Corneille, Molière, Pascal, and the eminent men of his day, including Boileau himself among the foremost. The kindly La Fontaine, taking sides with the learned Huet in the quarrel, didn't notice that despite his inadvertence he was on the eve of awakening to classic status himself.[3]

The best definition is example. Ever since France has had its age of Louis XIV and been able to contemplate it at some distance of time, she has understood what it is to be classical better than by any arguments. The eighteenth century, even in its miscellaneousness, added to this conception by some fine works produced by its four great men. Read *Le Siècle de Louis XIV* by Voltaire, *La Grandeur et la décadence des Romaines* by Montesquieu, *Les Epoques de la nature* by Buffon, *Le Vicaire savoyard* and the lovely pages of reverie and natural description by Jean-Jacques Rousseau, and then say whether the eighteenth century, in its more memorable aspects, did not know how to reconcile tradition with freedom of development and independence.[4] But at the beginning of the present century and under the Empire, in the face of the first attempts at a decidedly new and somewhat venturesome literature, among a few unyielding spirits rather more peevish than austere, the idea of the classical was to be oddly contracted and narrowed. The first dictionary of the academy (1694)[5] defined a classical author simply as "a highly

3. Sainte-Beuve refers here to the famous quarrel between the ancients and the moderns. Boileau's angry protest came when Charles Perrault read his poem *Le Siècle de Louis le Grand* before the French Academy in 1687. In it, as in his later *Parallèle des anciens et des modernes*, Perrault exalted the literature and learning of his own day and nation above those of ancient Greece and Rome. Pierre-Daniel Huet (1630–1721), a learned prelate and member of the academy, argued for the ancients.

4. Moralist, poet, dramatist, tale writer, indefatigable correspondent, Voltaire also tried his hand at history, as in the highly personal account of Louis XIV's reign mentioned here. Montesquieu published his *Considérations sur les causes de la grandeur des Romaines et de leur décadence* in 1734. But his reputation rests rather on *De l'esprit des lois* (1748), one of the greatest political treatises of the century, which influenced both the French Revolution and the Constitution of the United States. The naturalist Georges Buffon (1707–88) is best remembered for his *Discours sur le style* (1753), mentioned below by Sainte-Beuve. *Les Epoques de la nature* (1779) was part of his massive *Histoire naturelle*. Rousseau's "Profession de foi du vicaire savoyard" appears in *Emile*, his novelistic treatise on education. The "lovely pages of reverie and natural description" is an apparent reference to the *Rêveries du promeneur solitaire*, which Rousseau wrote late in life.

5. The *Dictionnaire* was a direct result of the original purpose of the academy

approved ancient author who is an authority in the subject he treats of." The 1835 dictionary of the academy tightens this definition considerably and in place of its slight vagueness makes it precise and even narrow. It defines as classical authors those "who have become *models* in whatever language"; and in all the articles that follow, the terms *models*, established *rules* for composition and style, *strict rules* to which one must *conform*, recur continually. This definition of *classic* was obviously made by the respectable members of the academy our predecessors, in the presence and view of what was then called the *romantic*, that is to say, in view of the enemy. The time has come, it seems to me, to renounce these restrictive and timid definitions and to broaden their spirit.

A true classic, as I should like to hear it defined, is an author who has enriched the human spirit, who has truly increased its treasure, who has caused it to take a step forward, who has discovered some unequivocal moral truth or laid fresh hold on some eternal passion in that heart where all seemed known and explored; who has conveyed his thought, his observation, or his discovery in whatever form, only let it be liberal and grand, choice and judicious, intrinsically wholesome and seemly; who has spoken to all men in a style of his own which at the same time turns out to be every man's style, a style that is new without neologism, at once new and old, easily contemporaneous with every age.

Such a classic may for a moment have been revolutionary, or at least have appeared so, but it is not. It did not begin by plundering round about it; it overturned whatever constrained it only in order speedily to restore the balance on the side of order and beauty.

If anyone should wish it, names can be listed under this definition, which I would deliberately make sweeping and unfixed, in a word, liberal. First I should put down the Corneille of *Polyeucte*, *Cinna*, and *Horace*. I should put down Molière, the most complete and most copious poetic spirit that we have had in French. "Molière is so great," said Goethe (that king of criticism),

---

founded in 1635 by Cardinal Richelieu to develop, unify, and purify the French language.

that he astounds us anew every time we read him. He is a man out of the ordinary; his plays approach the tragic, and no one dares to try to imitate them. His *Avare*, in which vice destroys all affection between the father and the son, is a work of the most sublime, and dramatic in the highest degree. . . . In a drama each of the actions must be important in itself and tend toward an even greater action. In this respect *Le Tartuffe* is a model. What an exposition the first scene is! From the outset everything has a lofty significance and gives promise of something much more important. The exposition in any play of Lessing's that one might méntion is very fine; but the one in *Tartuffe* is unique in the world. It is the greatest of its kind. . . . Every year I read a Molière play, just as every now and then I contemplate some engraving after the great Italian masters.[6]

I am not unaware that the definition of the classical that I have just given goes somewhat beyond the conception people usually have of this term. Included in it above all are the qualities of regularity, wisdom, moderation, and reason, dominating and comprising all the rest. Praising M. Royer-Collard, M. de Rémusat[7] said: "If he derives from our classical writers his *purity of taste, propriety of diction, variety of phrase*, his careful attention to *the matching of expression and thought*, the character he gives to these qualities is his alone." Here we see that the role assigned to the classical virtues seems primarily related to decorum and nuance, to stylistic adornment and restraint; this is also the common opinion. In this sense the finest classics would be writers of middle rank, correct, sensible, elegant, always clear, yet of noble passion and delicately veiled power. Marie-Joseph Chénier has summed up the poetics of these restrained and accomplished writers in these lines, in which he shows himself to be their worthy disciple:

> C'est le bon sens, la raison qui fait tout,
> Vertu, génie, esprit, talent et goût.
> Qu'est-ce vertu? raison mise en pratique;

6. These remarks of Goethe on Molière are taken from *Conversations with Eckermann*.

7. Charles de Rémusat (1797–1875) was a minor literary critic and historian of philosophy.

Talent? raison produite avec éclat;
Esprit? raison qui finement s'exprime;
Le goût n'est rien qu'un bon sens délicat;
Et le génie est la raison sublime.[8]

In writing these lines he was obviously thinking of Pope and Boileau, and of Horace, the master of them all. The essence of this theory, which subordinates the imagination and the sensibility itself to the reason, and of which Scaliger[9] was perhaps the first modern exponent, is, strictly speaking, the *Latin* theory, and it has also by long-standing preference been the *French* theory. Properly employed, without misconceiving the term *reason*, there is some truth in it. But obviously it *is* misconceived: if the reason can conform to the poetic spirit and be made one with it in a moral epistle, for example, surely it cannot be identical with that spirit, so varied and diversely creative, in the expression of the human passions in a play or an epic poem. In Dido's amorous rage in Book 4 of the *Aeneid*, or in Phèdre's ravings, where will you find anything like reason? In any case the intellectual temper that inspired this theory conduces to placing in the highest classical rank those writers who restrained their passion rather than those who have given it freer rein; to placing Virgil in that rank more assuredly than Homer, Racine rather than Corneille. The masterpiece which this theory loves to cite, which really unites all the qualifications of prudence, power, and mounting boldness, is *Athalie*. Turenne in his last two campaigns[10] and Racine in *Athalie* are the two mighty instances of what the wise and prudent can achieve when they are in full possession of their genius and at the utmost of their daring.

In his discourse on style, Buffon, laying stress on that unity of

8. "Good sense and reason comprise all else, / Moral force, genius, wit, talent, and taste. / What is moral force? reason applied. / Talent? reason manifested with brilliance. / Wit? reason in apt expression. / Taste is only subtle good sense, / And genius a sublime reason." This passage appears in "La Raison," one of the *Discours en vers* by Marie-Joseph Chénier (1764–1811), dramatist, poet, and politician.

9. Julius Caesar Scaliger (1484–1558) was an Italian-French rhetorician and classical scholar whose influential *Poetics* appeared in 1561.

10. Brilliant military tactician, Henri, vicomte de Turenne (1611–75) won distinction in France's wars with Spain and, later, the German Rhineland states.

design, arrangement, and execution which is the stamp of truly classical works, has said: "Every subject is one, and *however vast it may be, it can be comprehended in a single treatise.* Interruptions, pauses, and divisions should be admitted only when treating different subjects or when, having to speak of large, intricate, and disparate matters, the operation of genius becomes suspended by the multiplicity of obstacles and constrained by the necessity of circumstances. Otherwise, many divisions, far from making a work more solid, destroy its unity; the book seems clearer to the reader, but the author's purpose remains obscure. . . ." And he continues his critique with Montesquieu's *Esprit des lois* in mind, that book basically excellent but put together piecemeal, into which the illustrious author, weary before he had finished, was unable to breathe his full inspiration or in some fashion pull all his material together. Yet I find it hard to believe that in this same passage Buffon was not also thinking by contrast of Bossuet's *Discours sur l'histoire universelle*, that subject at once so vast and so much *one*, which the great orator was able so entirely to "comprehend in a single treatise." Let anyone open the first edition of this work, that of 1681, before the division into chapters, introduced later on and moved from the margin into the text, thereby cutting it up. The whole thing unfolds in a single unbroken movement, almost at a single breath, and you would think that here the orator has acted like the nature Buffon speaks of, that "he has worked according to an eternal plan, whence he has strayed at no point," so much does he seem to have penetrated in advance into the secrets and councils of Providence.

*Athalie* and the *Discours sur l'histoire universelle*—these are the loftiest masterpieces which strict classical theory can present to its friends and enemies alike. And yet, despite how much of the admirably simple and majestic goes into the production of such unique works, we should like, as is usual with art, to stretch it a little and to show that there is room to broaden it without going so far as to relax it completely. Goethe, whom I like to cite on questions like this, has said:

> I call the classic *healthy*, the romantic *sick*. For me, the poem of the *Niebelungen* is classical like Homer; both are in good health and

vigorous. Modern works are not romantic because they are new but
because they are weak, ailing, or infirm. Ancient works are not classical
because they are old but because they are vigorous, fresh, and hardy.
If we would consider the romantic and the classical from these two
viewpoints, we should all soon be in agreement.[11]

Indeed, I should like every liberal-minded person, before finally
making up his mind on this matter, first to make his own literary
world tour and regale himself with the spectacle of the several
literatures in their pristine vigor and infinite variety. What would
he see? Homer first of all, the father of the classical world, but who
is himself less certainly a simple individual than the vast and lively
expression of an entire epoch and semibarbarous civilization. In
order to make him a classic in the strict sense of the word, he had to
be endowed, after the event, with a design, a plan, with literary
intentions, and qualities of Atticism and urbanity which he surely
never dreamed of in the exuberant flowering of his natural gifts.
And at the side of Homer, what else appears? August and venerable
ancients, figures like Aeschylus and Sophocles, but all mutilated,
standing there only to give us some notion of their own ruins, the
remains of so many others probably as worthy as themselves of
having survived but who succumbed forever to the assaults of time.
This thought alone should instruct a judicious person against a too
simple and restricted conception of the whole of literature, even of
classical literature; he would see that that order, so regular and
restrained, that has since prevailed is only something artificially
made up out of our admiration of the past.

And what do we see when we come to the modern world? The
greatest figures we glimpse at the dawn of modern literatures are
those who upset and offend the best established of the restricted
ideas entertained about the beautiful and the seemly in poetry. Is
Shakespeare a classic, for example? Yes, today he is, for England
and for the world; but in Pope's time he was not. Pope and his
friends were the only outstanding classics, and they were regarded
as such by the generation that followed them. Today they are still
classics, and deserve to be, but they are classics of the second rank

11. From *Conversations with Eckermann.*

only, and there they remain, overtopped and relegated to their proper place by him who has reoccupied his own on the heights of the skyline.

I would be the last to speak ill of Pope or of his excellent disciples either, least of all when, like Goldsmith, they are possessed of artless good nature. Next to the very greatest, these are perhaps the most engaging of writers and poets, best able to lend charm to life. One day when Lord Bolingbroke was writing to Dr. Swift, Pope added a postscript to his letter, in which he said: "I fancy if we three were together but for three years, some good might be done even upon this age." [12] No, we must never speak lightly of men who could speak of themselves in this fashion without bragging; we ought rather to envy the lucky and favored ages in which talented men could think of such collaborations, which in those days were not fanciful. Those times, whether named after Louis XIV or Queen Anne, constitute the only truly classical period offering a propitious climate and shelter to perfected talents. We are all too well aware of this fact, we who live in disjointed times in which talents possibly equal to those of the past are spoiled and frittered away in an uncertain and inclement moral climate. Still, let us grant to every kind of greatness its share of superiority. The true sovereign men of genius triumph over difficulties where others fail; Dante, Shakespeare, and Milton managed to attain the full height of their genius and to produce their imperishable works in spite of obstacles, oppression, and disorders. There has been a lot of discussion about Byron's opinion of Pope, and people have tried to explain that species of contradiction by which the bard of *Don Juan* and of *Childe Harold* extolled the purely classical school and declared it to be the only good one, while writing so differently himself. Once again it is Goethe who spoke the truth about it when he observed that Byron, so great in the resources of poetic energy, was afraid of Shakespeare, more powerful than he was in the creation and staging of characters. "He had to repudiate him; that elevation so devoid of egoism bothered him; he sensed that he would be unable to spread himself at ease in its neighborhood. He never repudiated

12. Pope's postscript appears in Bolingbroke's letter to Swift conjecturally dated March 1731/32.

Pope because he wasn't afraid of him; he well knew that Pope was a wall beside him."[13]

If, as Byron wished, the school of Pope had retained its supremacy and a kind of literary empire in the past, Byron would have been first and unrivaled in his genre. The height of Pope's wall screened the mighty figure of Shakespeare from view, whereas, Shakespeare being enthroned and predominant in all his loftiness, Byron is only second.

In France, we had no great classic before the age of Louis XIV. The Dantes and Shakespeares, those pristine authorities to whom men recur sooner or later in moments of literary emancipation, are lacking to us. We have had only the rough drafts of great poets, such as Mathurin Regnier, or Rabelais, without visionary quality, without the passion and the gravity that make for consecration. Montaigne was a kind of protoclassic, of the family of Horace, but lacking worthy surroundings he gave himself up like a lost child to every fancy of his pen and temperament. The result is that we French less than any other people have been able to find among our ancestral authors anything entitling us to make, at certain moments, a bold reassertion of our literary liberties and immunities, and so it has been harder for us to remain classical while still asserting our literary freedom. However, with Molière and La Fontaine among our classics of the great age, no legitimate aspiration can be refused to those who have the daring and the skill.

The important thing today, it seems to me, is to maintain the conception and creed, while at the same time broadening it. There is no recipe for making classics; this fact must finally be recognized as self-evident. To believe that by imitating certain qualities of purity, sobriety, correctness, and elegance, regardless of personal inspiration and even of individual temperament, one can become classical is to believe that after Racine the elder must come Racine the younger—a respectable and melancholy role, the worst there is in poetry. What is more, it is not good to be regarded too quickly from the very outset as a classic by one's contemporaries, for then there is great risk of not remaining a classic for posterity. In his own day Fontanes appeared a pure classic to his friends; yet see how he faded after twenty-five years. How numerous are these precocious

13. From *Conversations with Eckermann.*

classics that do not hold up and are "classic" for a brief time only!
One fine morning you look back, surprised to find them no longer
standing erect behind you. Some of them, Madame de Sévigné
would blithely say, were "too good to last." With classics, the most
unexpected are still the best and greatest. Seek them preferably at
the hands of those virile geniuses truly born immortal and forever
flourishing. In appearance, the least classic of the four great poets
of Louis XIV's reign was Molière. He was applauded much more
than he was esteemed; people relished him without realizing his
worth. Next after Molière, La Fontaine seemed to be the least
classical. And now two centuries later we see what both of these men
have become. Are they not today, much above Boileau and even
above Racine, unanimously recognized as the richest and most
fertile in strokes of universal morality?

Moreover, there is really no question of sacrificing or disparaging
anything. The Temple of Taste, I think, needs to be rebuilt; but in
rebuilding it we have only to enlarge it, that it may become the
Pantheon of mankind's best, of all those who have made a notable
and lasting contribution to the store of the spirit's treasures and
delights. Since I myself (as is all too evident) have not the slightest
claim to being an architect or building contractor of temples, I shall
confine myself to expressing a few wishes, to submitting a competi-
tive bid, so to speak. First of all, I would exclude no worthy can-
didate, but assure each one his place, from that freest of creative
geniuses and greatest of unconscious classics, Shakespeare, down to
the least of the miniature classics, Andrieux.[14] "In my Father's
house are many mansions"[15]—let this be as true of the realm of

14. François Andrieux (1759–1833) was a lawyer, playwright, and professor of
literature who defended a strict classicism against the new romanticism of the early
nineteenth century.

15. Goethe, who is so favorable to the free diversity of genius and considers
every development legitimate so long as it attains the end of art, has ingeniously
compared Parnassus to Monserrat in Catalonia, which is or was entirely inhabited
by hermits and where every crag contained its holy anchorite. "Parnassus," he
said, "is a Monserrat that accommodates a number of establishments at its various
levels; let everyone go and look about him and he will find some spot to his liking,
whether it be a summit or some nook in the rocks." [Sainte-Beuve]

Cf. note 8, p. 21, above.

beauty here below as of the heavenly kingdom above. There, as always and everywhere, Homer would be foremost, most resembling a god. But behind him, like the procession of the three Wise Men of the East, would be seen those three magnificent poets, those three Homers long unknown to us, who also composed epic poems, prodigious and venerated works done in the manner of the ancient Asian folk: the Hindu poets Valmiki and Vyasa, and the Persian Firdausi.[16] In the realm of taste it is well to be at least aware that there are such men, and not to split up the human race. Having paid this homage to what needs only to be noticed and recognized, we would make no further excursions beyond our horizons, within which our eyes would be delighted by a thousand pleasing and imposing sights, regaled by a thousand varied and surprising discoveries, whose apparent confusion, however, would never be without harmony and accord. The most ancient sages and bards, those who reduced moral philosophy to maxims and sang it in simple strains, would be conversing among themselves in language choice and sweet; nor would they be astonished to find that they could understand each other from the very first word. The Solons, Hesiods, Theognises,[17] Jobs, Solomons—and why not Confucius too?—would welcome the most ingenious moderns, the La Rochefoucaulds and La Bruyères, who would say to each other after listening to these ancients: "They knew all that we know, and by bringing human experience up to date we have discovered nothing new." On the hill in nearest view and of gentlest slope, Virgil, in company with Menander, Tibullus, Terence, and Fénelon, would be engaged in conversations of rare delight and sacred charm, his mild features touched by a ray of light and tinged with modesty, as on that day when he entered the theater in Rome just after a recital of some of his verses and the entire audience rose before him as if by a unanimous impulse, paying him the same homage as they would to Augustus himself. Not far away from Virgil, regretful at being separated from so dear a friend, Horace would be presiding

16. Valmiki and Vyasa were the composers, or compilers, of the great Sanskrit epics *Ramayana* (ca. 300 B.C.) and *Mahabharata* (ca. A.D. 400), respectively. The epic poet Firdausi (ca. 935–1020) composed the Persian epic *Shahnama*.

17. Theognis was a sixth-century B.C. Greek poet.

(as far as so fastidious a poet and sage can be imagined as *presiding*) over the poets of civil life and those skilled at making good talk of the same subjects they sang in verse. Here would be Pope and Boileau, the one become less irritable, the other less grumbling. Montaigne, that poet at heart, would be here, to keep this charming group from giving the slightest impression of constituting a "literary school." Here too the self-regardless La Fontaine would be found, and, henceforth less flighty, here he would forever remain. Voltaire would wander by, but, though pleased by the sight of them, would lack the patience to stay. On the same hill with Virgil, a little lower down, Xenophon would be seen, his simple manner giving no hint of the military leader and suggesting rather a priest of the Muses, gathering around him the Attic spirits of every tongue and nation, the Addisons, Pellissons, and Vauvenargues,[18] all those who know the value of easy persuasion, of exquisite simplicity, and the blending of a sweet nonchalance with adornment. In the central spot three great men would like to meet frequently before the portico of the main temple (for there would be more than one temple within the enclosure). And when these three were together, no fourth, however great he might be, would think of joining in their talk or their silence, so great a measure of beauty would appear in them, and of moderation in greatness, and that perfection of harmony that occurs but once, in the world's first youth. Their three names have become the ideal of art: Plato, Sophocles, and Demosthenes. And yet after all, having made due obeisance to these demigods, do you not see over there a numerous and familiar throng of excellent spirits who will always prefer to follow the Cervanteses and the Molières, the practical painters of life, indulgent friends who are yet the best of benefactors, who captivate the whole man by laughter, gaily pour out all experience before him, and understand the powerful effect of a sane, hearty, and honest joy. I don't wish to prolong

18. Paul Pellisson (1624–93) was historiographer to Louis XIV. The *Maximes* of Luc de Vauvenargues (1715–47) express a moral optimism that sets them in contrast to those of La Rochefoucauld. Like the other groupings depicted in this *causerie*, Sainte-Beuve's association of these two French writers with the affable and urbane author of the *Spectator* illustrates his theory of *familles d'esprit*, the idea that writers can be divided into "families," that is, types of mind, style, or attitude uniting them across differences of period, nation, religion, and genre.

here a description which, were it complete, would comprise a whole book. The Middle Ages and Dante, be assured, would occupy sacred heights. At the feet of the singer of Paradise, almost all Italy would be spread out like a garden; there Boccaccio and Ariosto would be disporting themselves, and Tasso would rediscover the orange grove of Sorrento. In general, each separate nation would have its nook apart, but the authors would take delight in wandering outside. They would stroll out to meet brothers and sisters in the most unlikely places. Lucretius, for example, would love to discuss with Milton the origin of the world and the ending of chaos; but, arguing each according to his own interpretation, they would agree only in their heavenly pictures of poetry and of nature.[19]

So much for the classics. The imagination of each reader will enable him to complete the sketch and even to choose the group he prefers. For choose one must, because the primary condition of good taste, after all has been understood, is to cease from endless voyaging and finally settle somewhere and take a stand. Nothing cloys and smothers taste more than voyages without end; the spirit of poetry is no wandering Jew. When I speak of taking a stand and making a final choice, however, my conclusion is not to imitate even those who please us most among our past masters. Let us be content to savor them, to enter deeply into their spirit and admire them, and —late arrivals as we are—let us at least try to be ourselves. In choosing, let us be guided by our own instincts. Let us have the sincerity of our own genuine thoughts and feelings; that much we can always do. To this let us add, what is more difficult, greatness of soul, and direct ourselves, if possible, toward some high-placed goal. And even while speaking our own tongue and submitting to the conditions of the age in which we are placed and from which we draw alike our strength and our failings, let us ask ourselves from time to time, as we raise our eyes to those hills and gaze upon those groups of revered mortals: "What would they say about us?"

19. The long hexameter poem *De rerum natura* [*On the Nature of Things*], by the first-century B.C. Roman philosopher-poet Lucretius, is the fullest extant discussion of the Epicurean atomic theory, which Sainte-Beuve here regards as an alternate poetic account of the Creation to that given in *Paradise Lost*.

But why speak always about being an author and writing? Happy are those who read, and reread, and in what they read can follow their own free inclinations! There comes a time in life when, all voyaging over and all experiences at an end, there is no greater joy than to study and probe more deeply into what we already know, to savor familiar tastes, like seeing again and again the people we love. These are the pure delights of heart and fancy in mature life. It is at this age that the word *classic* takes on its true meaning and defines itself for every man of taste by the irresistible predilection of his choice. By this time taste has been fully formed and determined; by now, if ever, our own good sense is consummated. We no longer have the time for effort or the desire to set forth on discoveries. We stick to our friends, to those tested by long experience. Old wine, old books, old friends. We say to ourselves, like Voltaire in these delicious lines:

> Jouissons, écrivons, vivons, mon cher Horace!
>
> . . . . . . . . . . . . . . . . . . . . . . . . .
> J'ai vécu plus que toi: mes vers dureront moins;
> Mais, au bord du tombeau, je mettrai tous mes soins
> A suivre les leçons de ta philosophie,
> A mépriser la mort en savourant la vie,
> A lire tes écrits pleins de grâce et de sens,
> Comme on boit d'un vin vieux qui rajeunit les sens.[20]

Finally, whether it be Horace or someone very different, whatever favorite author gives us back our own thoughts ripened and enriched, we shall then seek from one of those fine old spirits an unfailing intercourse, a friendship that never declines and cannot fail us, and that habitual stamp of serenity and grace which reconciles us, as we so often have need of being reconciled, with mankind and with ourselves.

*Causeries du lundi*, III, 38–55 (October 21, 1850).

20. "Let us write, live, and enjoy ourselves, dear Horace! / . . . / I have lived longer than you; my verses will not last so long as yours. / Yet, as I near the grave, I shall constantly try / To abide by the lessons of your philosophy, / To taste of life while scorning death, / And to read yóur poems so full of grace and good sense, / As one quaffs an old wine that restores vitality." The lines are from Voltaire's "Epitre CXI: à Horace" (1771). Sainte-Beuve has omitted four lines from the quoted section.

# Rousseau's *Confessions*

*In few of his essays are Sainte-Beuve's talents as historian, psychologist, and appreciative critic more happily combined than in this close study of the* Confessions. *His central concern is with Rousseau as literary artist and with the revitalization of French prose which he effected. But the stylistic analysis is referable at every point both to the personality and experience—the unique sensibility—of Rousseau himself and to the literary climate of his time and place.*

Having spoken[1] of the pure, light, unemphatic language, entirely free-flowing and facile, which the waning seventeenth century partly bequeathed to the eighteenth, today I should like to speak of that eighteenth-century language as it appears in the writer who did most to modernize it or at any rate subjected it to the greatest revolution since Pascal, a revolution from which we of the nineteenth century take our date. Before Rousseau, even as early as Fénelon, many manners of writing had been tried which were no longer those of the pure seventeenth century: Fontenelle had his manner, if ever there was one, and so did Montesquieu, a manner stronger, solider, and more striking, but a manner nonetheless. Voltaire alone affected no manner; his lively, clear, rapid utterance was poured out from very near the source, as it were. "You see," he writes somewhere, "that I express myself quite clearly; I am like small brooks that are transparent because they are not very deep." He said this with a smile, as we often express such half-truths to ourselves. The age, however, demanded something more. It longed to be moved, excited, and rejuvenated by the expression of ideas and feelings it imperfectly conceived and was still groping for. The prose

1. In his *causerie* of the previous week, on Madame de Caylus.

of Buffon in the first volume of the *Histoire naturelle* offered something
of what it desired, but more majestic than lively, somewhat beyond
its reach and too limited by its scientific subject matter. Then came
Rousseau. The day of his full self-discovery disclosed to the age the
writer best qualified to express, with novelty, vigor, and impassioned
logic, the indistinct ideas then stirring in the womb of time and
awaiting birth. In possessing himself of that language which he had
to overcome and subdue, he slightly strained it, giving it a bend it
was thereafter never to lose. But this impairment was more than
outweighed by his contribution, for in many respects he rejuvenated
the language and gave it new vigor. Since Rousseau, our best
writers have embodied their innovations in the language which he
created and formed and they have tried to improve upon. For men
of taste, the pure style of the seventeenth century, as we like to
recall it, was now hardly more than a graceful and fondly remembered bit of antiquity.

Although the *Confessions* was not published until after Rousseau's
death, when his influence was already firmly established, it is in
this work that we can most readily study both the fine qualities and
the deficiencies of his talent. This we shall try to do, as much as
possible limiting our attention to Rousseau the writer, yet without
entirely ruling out of consideration the ideas and character of
Rousseau the man. The present moment is not very favorable to
Rousseau, who is regarded as having created and fostered many of
the evils which are currently afflicting us. "No writer," it has been
judiciously observed, "is more calculated to make the poor arro-
gant." Nevertheless, as we consider him here we shall try to resist
that rather subjective attitude that inclines well-disposed people to
bear him a grudge in these trying times through which we are living.
Men of his significance and extensive influence are not to be judged
by the emotional reactions of a passing moment.

The idea of writing *Confessions* seems so natural to Rousseau and
so congenial to his temperament and talent that one would hardly
suppose he needed the prompting of a suggestion. The idea first
came to him, however, from his publisher in Amsterdam, Rey, and
then from Duclos as well. In 1764, at the age of fifty-two, having
produced the *Nouvelle Héloise* and *Emile*, Rousseau began to draft his

*Confessions* after his departure from Montmorency and during his stay at Motiers, Switzerland. Recently, in the last number of the *Revue suisse* (October, 1850), there appeared a first draft of the *Confessions* taken from a manuscript deposited in the Neuchâtel library, a first rough sketch which he later suppressed. This original beginning, far less emphatic and pompous than that which now forms the opening pages of the *Confessions*, contains no "trumpet blast of the Last Judgment"; nor does it end with the famous apostrophe to the "Eternal Being." In it Rousseau sets forth at much greater length, but in a philosophic way, his intention to describe himself and make his confessions with unsparing honesty. He makes clear exactly wherein the originality and uniqueness of his project lie.

> No one can write a man's life except the man himself. His inner mode of being, his genuine life, is known only to himself. But in writing it he dissembles it, giving the title of biography to what is really an apology: he shows himself as he would like to appear, not at all as he is. The frankest are truthful at most in what they say but they lie by their silences, and what they suppress so very much changes what they pretend to confess that in telling us only a part of the truth they really tell us nothing. I place Montaigne at the head of these "sham-sincere" persons who wish to deceive us while telling the truth. The only faults they ascribe to themselves are quite amiable ones, *although no man ever existed without some faults that were odious.* Montaigne paints us his likeness, but in profile only. Who knows whether some scar on his cheek or a deformed eye on the side of his face hidden from view may not have entirely altered his facial expression?

Thus he aims to do what no one before has thought of doing or dared to do. As for the style, he thinks he will have to invent one as novel as his project, one suited to the diversity and disparity of the things he means to describe:

> If like those before me I set out to produce a work carefully composed, I shall show myself with make-up on, not give a plain portrait. I am trying to portray myself, not make a book. I shall be working in a *camera obscura*, so to speak, with no need of any other art than simply following the contours I see outlined there. Therefore I handle my style

as I handle my material. I shall not try to make it uniform but rather accept it as it comes and change it according to my mood, without scruple. I shall express everything just as I feel it and see it, without refinement or painstaking, never troubling myself about incongruities. Yielding myself at the same time to the memory of the impression received and to my present feeling, I shall render a dual portrait of my soul, namely, as it was at the moment the event happened and as it is at the moment I am describing it. My natural, uneven style, sometimes rapid, sometimes diffuse, sometimes wise and sometimes mad, now grave, now gáy, will itself make part of my story. In short, however it may be with the style of this work, for its subject it will always be a book valuable to philosophers. It is, I repeat, a guide to the study of the human heart, *the only such guide in existence.*

Rousseau's error lay not in believing that by confessing himself aloud to us in this way, and with a feeling so different from Christian humility, he was doing something unique or even something very suggestive for the study of the human heart; his error lay in believing he was doing something *useful.* He failed to see that what he was doing was as if a doctor should set about explaining in a clear, fascinating manner, for the use of the fashionable and the uninstructed, some well-characterized mental disease. Such a doctor would be culpable, and in part responsible for all the maniacs and madmen his book would make through imitation and contagion.

The opening pages of the *Confessions* are too emphatic and rather labored. Right at the outset I come on "void *occasioned* by a lapse of memory," and he uses expressions like the "authors of his days. . . ." This sort of thing is distasteful and has nothing of that flower of expression whose fragrance we were relishing the other day under the name of urbanity.[2] Yet notice, immediately alongside these dictional crudities and rusticities, what an original simplicity we also find, so searching and intimate!

I felt before I thought. This is the common lot of mankind, which I experienced more than most. I cannot recall what I did before the age of five or six. I do not know how I learned to read; I recall only

2. Another reference to the *causerie* on Madame de Caylus, in which Sainte-Beuve defines *urbanity* as "not only an excellence of language and intellect, but also a kind of social and moral virtue that renders a man pleasing to others and embellishes and confirms the commerce of life."

my earliest reading and how it affected me. . . . My mother had left some novels which my father and I betook ourselves to reading after supper. At first the idea was merely to train me by the reading of interesting books, but soon our interest became so lively that we took turns reading without letup, and so we spent our evenings. We could not stop until we had reached the end of the book. Sometimes my father, hearing the first twitterings of the morning swallows, would say, overcome with shame, "Let's go to bed; I'm even more childish than you."

Note well that swallow. It is the first one, and herald of a new springtime in our language, of that feeling for nature which in the eighteenth century begins for us French only with Rousseau. With him also there arises in our literature the affection for domestic life, that bourgeois life, poor, sequestered, and cosy, in which so many treasures of virtue and tenderness abound. There are some unpleasant details about stealing "victuals" we can overlook for that old song of childhood of which he now remembers only the tune and a few disconnected words, but is always trying to recapture. Old as he is, he never thinks of it without being moved by its charm. "It's a humor I do not pretend to understand," he tells us,

> but it is absolutely impossible for me to sing it all the way through without being stopped by my tears. A hundred times I've been on the point of writing to Paris for the rest of the words, on the chance someone might still know them; but I am almost sure that the pleasure I get in recalling this tune would partly disappear if I had evidence that other people besides my poor Aunt Suzy had sung it.

This is what is really new in the author of the *Confessions*, the thing that delights us by opening up unforeseen sources of intimate, homely sensibility. The other day we were looking at the *Souvenirs* of Madame de Caylus. But what childhood memories does she tell us about? What did she dote on? What did she weep over when she left the house where she was born and brought up? Would she so much as dream of telling us these things? Those refined aristocratic types, so endowed with exquisite good taste and a lively sense of mockery, either never loved these simple things or never dared to show it. Their intellects we know and these too we take pleasure in; but where are their hearts? In order to show oneself thus subject to inner, natural feelings, one must be of the middle class, from the provinces, and—like Rousseau—a "new man."

And so, when we somewhat regretfully observe that Rousseau strained and, as it were, ploughed and harrowed the language, we quickly add that he fertilized it and enriched it with a new seed at the same time.

A man of the proud aristocratic breed but a disciple of Rousseau with scarcely more sense or fear of ridicule than Rousseau himself, M. de Chateaubriand, repeated in *René* and in his *Mémoires* this more or less direct manner of self-avowal and confession, turning it to magical and surprising effects. But notice the difference. Rousseau lacks the innate loftiness; he is not exactly—indeed, far from it!—what is called a "well-born" child. He has a hankering after vice, and low vice at that; he has shameful secret lusts that do not bespeak noble birth. He is subject to those long periods of bashfulness that suddenly break out into the impudences of a "scamp" and "rogue," as he calls himself. In short, he lacks that safeguard of honor which M. de Chateaubriand had, from his earliest childhood, standing watch like an alert sentinel over his shortcomings. Still, with all these disadvantages which, following his example, we do not shrink from calling by their rightful names, Rousseau is superior to Chateaubriand in the sense that he is more human, more of a man endowed with human feelings. He has nothing of Chateaubriand's incredible austerity (an austerity truly feudal) or of his lapses of feeling in speaking of his father and mother, for example. When he comes to the faults of his father, a plain man but given to pleasure and unsteady, who remarries and abandons Rousseau to his fate, with what good taste he alludes to this painful circumstance! With what imaginative sympathy he treats it! I do not mean chivalrous fastidiousness; I mean a genuinely felt delicacy which is moral and human.

It is incredible that this inner moral sense with which Rousseau was furnished and which kept him on such good terms with other men should not have made him aware of how far he forfeited it on many occasions of his life and in many of the expressions he indulges in his writings. His style, like his life itself, is somewhat infected by the vices of his early education and the bad company he first frequented. After a childhood spent decently in the bosom of his family, he is apprenticed and undergoes hardships that spoil his good breeding and vitiate his delicacy of feeling. Words like *polisson*, *vaurien*, *gueux*, *fripon* [scamp, wretch, ragamuffin, swindler] do not in the least repel him and even seem to flow repeatedly with a certain complaisance from his pen. His language always retained something of the ill breeding of his early years. In Rousseau's work I distinguish two kinds of linguistic debasement: one stems only from his provincial origins and from his speaking the French of a man born outside of France. Without batting an eye he will write, *"Comme que je fasse,"* or *"Comme que ce fût,"* instead of *"De quelque manière que je fasse," "De quelque manière que ce fût,"* and so forth ["However I did"; "however it was . . ."]. He articulates forcefully and harshly, sometimes sounding like a man with a goiter. But this defect can be forgiven him, since in many happy pages he succeeded so well in triumphing over it and by dint of hard work and profound feeling his voice was rendered more flexible and he was able to bring mildness and a seeming artlessness into his pedantic and crabbed prose style. The other species of debasement and corruption noticeable in him is more serious, since it relates to the moral sense. It seems beyond doubt that there are certain things that should not be expressed, certain ignoble, disgusting, cynical expressions which a decent man simply does without. At one time or another Rousseau was a lackey, a fact detectable in his style in more than one passage. He disrelishes neither the word nor the condition. "If Fénelon were living you would be a Catholic," Bernardin de Saint-Pierre[3] said to him one day when he was visibly moved by some part of the worship service. "Oh!" cried Rousseau with tears streaming down his face, "if Fénelon were still living I would try to become his lackey in order to become worthy of being his *valet de chambre*." Even in his emotions the lack of good taste is unmistakable. Rousseau is not only a mechanic of language, who was an apprentice before becoming a master and whose work shows traces here and there of the soldering; in his moral nature he is a man who while still young underwent the most miscellaneous experiences, and whose sensi-

3. Jacques-Henri Bernardin de Saint-Pierre (1737–1814) is best known for his idyllic novel *Paul et Virginie*.

bility is not pained when he mentions certain vile and ugly things. I shall say no more on this deep-rooted vice, this stain which it is distressing to have to confront and deplore in so great a writer and painter, in a man of Rousseau's stature.

Slow to think and quick to feel, burning with suppressed desires and uneasy in the fetters of daily existence, Rousseau reaches the age of sixteen. He describes himself as follows:

> I attained my sixteenth year, restive, discontented with everything and with myself, with no relish of my condition and none of the pleasures of my age, eaten up with desires whose object I did not know, weeping for no reason, sighing without knowing for what; in short, cherishing my illusions because nothing I saw around me was so precious as they. On Sunday my friends called on me after church to play with them. I would gladly have avoided them if I could; but, once at play in their company, I threw myself into the games more intensely than anyone else. *I was hard to pry loose and then hard to hold back.*

Always in extremes! In this passage we immediately recognize the first formulation of the thoughts of René, and in almost the same words, those words that have already become a strain of music sounding in our ears:

> My temperament was impetuous, my character unstable. By turns ardent and joyous, taciturn and cast down, I gathered about me my young companions; then, suddenly leaving them, I sat down apart by myself to contemplate the hurrying clouds or listen to the sound of the rain in the leaves. . . .

And again:

> While still young I cultivated the Muses; in the freshness of its passions there is nothing more poetic than the heart of a sixteen-year-old. The morning of life is like the morning of the day, full of purity, images, and harmony.[4]

4. For Sainte-Beuve, François de Chateaubriand's fictional hero René best typifies the element of extreme individualistic sensitivity in romantic literature, whose origins he ascribes directly to Rousseau. The two quotations are from *René*, a section of *Génie du Christianisme* (1802) which Chateaubriand republished separately in 1805.

René, in fact, is none other than this young man of sixteen transposed from his native element into other natural surroundings and conditions: no longer an apprentice engraver, the son of a Genevan bourgeois of the lowest class, but a widely traveled young nobleman infatuated with the Muses. At first glance it all seems bathed in more alluring and poetic colors; the unexpected landscape and setting enhance the personality and bespeak a novel manner. But the original type of the sensitive soul is just where we have located it, and it is Rousseau who first discovered it, by looking within himself.

René presents us a more flattering model because in him all the base aspects of human nature are hidden from view; the various hues of the Hellenic, of chivalry, and of Christianity mingle in him to appear on the surface of his personality. In this masterpiece of art words have taken on a fresh magic; they are words replete with light and harmony. In every direction the horizon has been broadened and is played upon by the rays of Olympus. At first sight Rousseau has nothing comparable to these qualities, but deep down he is truer, more real, more alive. This workingman's child who goes out to play with his companions after church service or to daydream alone when he can, this well-formed little adolescent of the lively glance and fine features who calls all things to account rather more than we could wish—he has more reality than René, and more life. He is more artless, passionate, and visceral. Both temperaments, René's and Rousseau's, have about them a touch of the sickly, an excess of ardor mingled with inactivity and idleness, an overplus of imagination and sensibility which becomes ingrown and self-destructive. But of the two Rousseau is the more genuinely sensitive, the more original and sincere in his flights of fancy, his vague longings, his depictions of an ideal of felicity granted and lost. At the end of the first book of the *Confessions*, when he is leaving his native land and calls up a simple and touching picture of the obscure happiness he could have enjoyed there; when he tells us: "In the bosom of my religion, country, family, and friends, I should have lived a sweet, peaceful life, such as my temperament required, in the constancy of an employment I enjoyed and in a society after my own heart; I should have been a good Christian, a good citizen, a good father, a good friend, a good worker, a good man in every respect; I should have loved my condition in life, *should perhaps have done it honor*, and, having lived a life obscure and simple but untroubled and agreeable, I should have died peacefully, surrounded by my own people; though no doubt soon forgotten, I should have been missed for as long as I was remembered"—when he speaks to us in this fashion, he really persuades us of the sincerity of his desire and regret, so much does his every word breathe a profound and lively feeling for the sweet, wholesome, untroubled charm of a private life.

So let us, who in this century have become more or less afflicted with this malady of daydreaming, not behave like newly created noblemen who deny their ancestry. Let us understand that before being the unworthy sons of the noble René we are more assuredly the grandsons of the bourgeois Rousseau.

The first book of the *Confessions* is not the most remarkable, but in it Rousseau stands already fully revealed, with his arrogance, his vices in embryo, his bizarre and grotesque moods, his base actions and his filthiness (you see I omit nothing); but also with his pride, and with that resiliency of independence and strength of purpose which compensate for them; with that happy, healthy childhood as well as that suffering and tormented adolescence which, predictably, will later prompt him to reproaches against society and vengeful retaliation; with his tender feeling for the domestic happiness he so little enjoyed; and, in addition to all else, with the first fragrant gusts of spring signaling that awakening to nature that was to burst forth in the literature of the nineteenth century. Nowadays we are too prone to be insensitive to these first picturesque pages of Rousseau. Our taste has become so cloyed with their colors that we forget how fresh and novel these first landscapes seemed at that time, and how significant an event was their first appearance in that highly sophisticated, ultrarefined but arid society, bereft in its very nature of that free-flowing sap which, each season, comes once again to flower. It was Rousseau who reinfused the puissant vegetable juices into the delicate dried-out tree. French readers, habituated to the artificial atmosphere of the salon, those *citified* readers as he called them, were surprised and delighted at the sensation of those fine cool mountain breezes blowing from the Alps to breathe new life into a literature as jejune as it was refined.

The time was ripe for this revitalization, and in this respect Rousseau must be considered not a corruptor of the language but, in the aggregate, a regenerator.

Before him in France only La Fontaine had had so deep an understanding and feeling for nature and for the charms of rustic musing. But his example had little effect; his contemporaries allowed the good fellow with his fables to go his own way while they remained in their salons. Rousseau was the first to induce the whole fashionable world to come out into the open air and abandon their tree-lined garden paths for rambles in the real countryside.

The beginning of the second book of the *Confessions* is delightful and thoroughly refreshing. Here for the first time we meet Madame de Warens. In her portrayal Rousseau's style becomes gracefully mellowed and subdued and at the same time reveals a certain trait, an essential vein in the man himself and in his total manner, namely, sensuality. "Rousseau," an able critic has said, "had a voluptuous mind." Women occupy a prominent place in his work; absent or present, they and their charms capture his attention; they inspire and move him, and something of their spirit pervades everything he writes. Of Madame de Warens he writes: "How, approaching for the first time in my life an amiable, polite, *dazzling* woman, a lady my social superior, whose equal I have never dealt with—how shall I find sufficient presence of mind to be sure of pleasing her?" This facility and ease of manner, which most of the time he hardly achieved in the actual presence of women, was always to be a mark of his prose style in describing them. The most lovable pages of the *Confessions* are those which relate his first meeting with Madame de Warens and again those in which he describes his welcome by Madame Basile, the pretty wife of the Turin merchant. "She was *resplendent* and richly dressed, and despite her gracious manner I was awed by her brilliance. But her most kindly welcome, her indulgent tone, and her gentle, affectionate manners soon put me at ease; I saw I was succeeding, and that made me succeed even more." In the lustrous tones of this description do you not catch something of the splendor of the Italian sunshine? And then he narrates that lively, wordless scene which no one can ever forget, that scene conducted in gestures, checked at just the right moment, full of blushings and young desires. Add to this the stroll near Annecy with Miss Galley and Miss Graffenried, every detail of which is delightful. Pages like these amounted to the discovery of a new world in French literature, a world of sunlit freshness which had all along lain nearby without anyone's having yet noticed it. They offered a blend of sensibility and natural simplicity in which the dash of sensuality was manifested only to the extent proper and necessary to liberate us at last from a false metaphysics of the heart and from conventional concepts of the human spirit. To this extent, descriptive sensuality cannot be displeasing; besides, it is moderate and undisguised, which makes it more innocent than the sensuality employed by many a painter since.

Generally speaking, Rousseau as a painter has the sense of *reality*. It is there whenever he speaks of beauty, which, even when it is imaginary like his Julie, takes on bodily and clearly visible forms, not that of an airy and intangible rainbow. This feeling for reality is such that he wants every scene he recalls or invents and every character he introduces to be set or to act in a specific locale of which every slightest detail might be graphically reproduced and preserved. One of the criticisms he levels against the great novelist Samuel Richardson is his failure to associate the memory of his characters with a locality which readers would delight to recognize in paintings. Notice how Rousseau was able to naturalize his own Julie and St. Preux[5] in the Pays-de-Vaud, on the shores of that lake around which he never ceased to wander in spirit. His accurate, steady mind everywhere lends its graving tool to the imagination, in order that nothing essential to the sketch be omitted. Finally, this sense of reality in Rousseau reveals itself in the very care with which, while recounting all his many doings, his adventures happy and unhappy, including the most wildly romantic, he never forgets to mention his meals, the details of a healthful, frugal fare fit to bring joy to heart and mind.

This feature too is an essential trait; it is part of that spirit of the

5. The young lovers in Rousseau's *La Nouvelle Héloïse* (1761), an epistolary novel, like Richardson's.

middle-class commoner that I noted in Rousseau. He had known what it was to be hungry and records in the *Confessions*, with a blessing to Providence, the last occasion when he literally felt misery and hunger. Moreover, not even in the idealized picture he was later to give of his happiness does he forget to make room for the things of real life and common humanity, for *visceral* things. It is for these many truthful aspects of his work, combined with his eloquence, that he claims and holds our attention.

Nature sincerely felt and loved for herself forms the basis of Rousseau's inspiration whenever that inspiration is wholesome, not morbid. When he revisits Madame de Warens after his return from Turin, he lives for a time in her house and from his chamber looks out on gardens and can see the open country. "This was the first time since Bossey" (the place where he was sent to boarding school during childhood), he writes, "that I could see *green outside my windows*." Until that moment it had been a matter of no account in French literature whether anyone saw any *green* before him or not; to Rousseau goes the credit of making us aware of it. From this point of view we might define him in a word: he is the first writer to "put some green" into our literature. Domiciled thus at the age of nineteen in the home of a beloved woman to whom however he does not dare declare his passion, Rousseau abandons himself to a sadness "which had yet nothing somber in it and could be alleviated by any flattering hope." One religious holiday when everyone is at vespers he takes a walk alone outside the city. "The sound of the bells," he writes,

> which always strangely affected me, the song of the birds, the beauty of the day, the sweetness of the countryside, the *scattered rustic* houses which I imagined might be our common abode, all these made such a lively, tender, sad, moving impression on me that I saw myself ecstatically transported to that happy time and happy abode where my heart, possessing all the felicity that could please it, relished it with ineffable delight, without so much as a thought of sensual pleasure.

Such were the feelings experienced at Annecy by the boy from Geneva in the year 1731, at a time when at Paris they were reading *Le Temple de Gnide*.[6] On that day he discovered reverie, a novel

6. An erotic essay by Montesquieu, published in 1725.

charm once dismissed as an eccentricity in La Fontaine, which Rousseau was about to bring once for all into a literature hitherto either elegant or matter-of-fact. Reverie—this was his innovation, his discovery, his personal America. That day's dream he realized some years later during his sojourn at Les Charmettes, when he took that walk on Saint-Louis's day which he has described as nothing like it had ever before been depicted:

> Everything seemed to conspire in the happiness of that day. Shortly before, it had rained; not a bit of dust and the *brooks running brim-full;* a fresh cool breeze fluttered the leaves, the air was pure, the horizon cloudless; serenity prevailed in the sky as in our hearts. We dined in a peasant's cottage, sharing our meal with his family, who gave us their kindhearted blessing. Such good folk are those poor Savoyards!

And he goes on, with these sentiments of kindliness, of close observation and unaffected truthfulness, to elaborate a painting in which all is perfection and delight, and only the name *Mama,* applied to Madame de Warens, grates painfully on our moral sensibilities.

This moment at Les Charmettes, where his young spirit was to bloom for the first time, is the most exquisite in the *Confessions,* and it was never again to be recaptured, not even when Rousseau retired to the Hermitage. In the description of those years at the Hermitage and the passionate feelings they brought him, there is still considerable allurement and perhaps more clarity of outline than in all that has gone before; nevertheless, he will have good reason to exclaim, "This place is no Les Charmettes!" The misanthropy and suspicion to which he is already subject will haunt him during this period of solitude. His thoughts will revert constantly to the world of Paris, the world of d'Holbach[7] and his circle; although he will enjoy his retreat in spite of them, the distraction will poison his dearest delights. During these years his temperament will become embittered and fall prey to an ailment from which it will never recover. True enough, then and until the end he is to know some delicious moments. On the isle of Saint-Pierre in the middle of

7. Baron Paul Henri d'Holbach (1723–89), a contributor to Diderot's *Encyclopédie* and prominent member of the group of *philosophes* that included Helvétius, d'Alembert, and Diderot himself.

Lake Bienne he will enjoy an interval of calm and forgetfulness which will inspire some of his finest pages, like that fifth Promenade of the *Rêveries*, which, along with the third Letter to Malesherbes,[8] must be ranked with the most exquisite passages of the *Confessions*. Nothing, however, was ever to equal the fresh, buoyant gaiety of his description of life at Les Charmettes. Rousseau's true happiness, the happiness of which no one, including himself, could deprive him, was his power of thus evoking and (with the striking precision that marked his recollections) retracing such scenes of his youth, something he was able to do even during the years when he was most troubled and beset.

The *voyage pédestre* [account of a walking tour], with its moment-by-moment impressions, was another of Rousseau's inventions, one of his novel contributions to literature which other writers have since much overworked. Although he enjoyed the first of these pedestrian journeys, it was only much later that it occurred to him to write down what he had experienced. Only then, he assures us, when he was "traveling on foot in fine weather through a beautiful countryside, unhurried," on the way to some agreeable object he was in no haste to reach—only then was he entirely himself, and ideas, cold and dead in the study, came alive and took wing in his consciousness.

> There is something about walking that animates and enlivens my thoughts; I can hardly think at all when I am settled at some spot; my body must be in motion for my mind to be set going. The sight of the countryside, the succession of pleasing views, the open air, a good appetite, the good health I get from walking, the freedom of a tavern, the distance from everything that makes me aware of my dependent state and reminds me of my station in life—all these set free my soul, lend great daring to my thought, throw me into the immensity of things, as it were, to combine, select, and make them mine as I please, without uneasiness or fear. I have all nature at my unbridled command. . . .

At moments like these one must not ask him to write down the thoughts sublime, mad, or genial that enter his mind; he prefers

8. Chrétien Guillaume de Malesherbes (1721–94) was a statesman friendly to the *philosophes* who aided the publication of the *Encyclopédie*.

relishing and enjoying their flavor to giving them expression. "Besides, did I bring along paper and pen? If I had thought of those things, nothing worth recording would have occurred to me. I did not foresee that I should have any ideas; they come when they please, not when I please." To take him at his word, then, in all that he has since recounted we should have only distant recollections and faint memories of what he was like on those occasions. And yet could anything be at once truer, more accurate, more delectable! Take for example that night spent outdoors on the banks of the Rhône, or the Saône, in a high-banked lane near Lyon.

> I lay down voluptuously on the shelf of a kind of recess or false door hollowed out of the terrace wall; the treetops formed a canopy for my bed; there was a nightingale directly over my head and I fell asleep listening to its song. My slumber was sweet and my waking sweeter. It was broad daylight. As soon as I opened my eyes I beheld the water, the green foliage, an admirable landscape. I rose and shook myself. Feeling hungry, I set out for the city determined to spend my remaining two small silver coins on a hearty breakfast.

All the essential Rousseau, his reverie, his idealism, his sense of reality, is in that passage. And those *two small silver coins*, coming right after the nightingale, provide just the right touch to bring us back to earth and let us feel all the humble enjoyment that attaches to poverty when it is joined to poetry and youth. I wanted to include this quotation about the silver coins in order to show that in Rousseau we have something not found in *René* or *Jocelyn*.[9]

In Rousseau, the picturesque is well balanced, steady, and lucid even when most piquant; the colors are always laid on a firmly sketched outline. In this respect, this citizen of Geneva is thoroughly French. If he does not always display the warmer light and unrelieved clarity of Italy or Greece; if, as around that lovely Lake Geneva, the north wind sometimes chills the air and a cloud may suddenly throw its grayish shadow on the mountain sides, there are days and hours of limpid and perfect serenity. Writers have since "improved upon" this style and thought they had surpassed and

9. *Jocelyn* is the first part of a long metaphysical poem by Alphonse de Lamartine (1790–1869).

eclipsed it; and as concerns a few effects of color and sound they have no doubt succeeded. Nonetheless, Rousseau's style is still the safest and least doubtful example we can cite in the area of modern literary innovation. In his case, the linguistic center is not too violently dislocated. His successors went farther, not only moving the seat of Empire to Byzantium but frequently carrying it off to Antioch and Central Asia. With them, sheer imaginative display absorbs and dominates everything else.

The portraits in the *Confessions* are lively, keen, and shrewd. His friend Bâcle, the musician Venture, the legal seer Simon are each artfully caught and closely studied. They are not so easily expunged as the portraits in *Gil Blas;*[10] rather they are indelibly engraved. In executing them Rousseau was mindful of his first trade.

In this brief survey of the author of the *Confessions* I have been able only to point to those aspects by which he remains a master and to pay homage on this occasion to the creator of reverie, the man who inoculated us with the feeling for nature and the sense of reality, the father of the literature which expresses private experience and portrays inner life. What a pity that it is alloyed by misanthropic pride and that so many charming substantial beauties are marred by a tone of cynicism. But these follies and vices of the man cannot prevail over his unique merits or conceal from our view the great qualities for which he continues to stand superior to his literary descendants.

*Causeries du lundi*, III, 78–97 (November 4, 1850).

10. *Gil Blas* is the picaresque novel by Alain René Le Sage (1668–1747).

# Madame Bovary

*One test of a critic's powers, one on which Sainte-Beuve is generally admitted to have scored poorly, is how soundly he judges his contemporaries. Modern admirers of Flaubert's masterpiece may complain that Sainte-Beuve's appraisal is only lukewarm, and hardly anyone will now take seriously his objection that Flaubert's fictional world is too unrelievedly depressing. Yet it is perhaps equally worth noting how unerringly, in praising the novel, the critic put his finger on certain aspects of it that have since become commonplaces of modern appreciation of Flaubert's performance: his conscious artistry and verbal economy, the matchless irony of the seduction scene at the agricultural fair, the brilliant satirical portrait of M. Homais.*

I have not forgotten that this work was the subject of a debate entirely other than literary,[1] but I am above all mindful of the conclusions and the wisdom of the judges. Henceforth the work belongs to art and to art alone; it is justiciable only by criticism, and criticism can use its full independence in discussing it.

It can do so and it should do so. We often go to great trouble to evoke bygone things, to revive ancient authors, works almost no one any longer reads, endowing them afresh with a glimmer of interest and a semblance of life. But when genuine living works pass within our range, under full press of sail and ensigns waving aloft as though to say, "What do you think of us?" if we are really critics, with a single drop in our veins of that blood which animated the Popes, Boileaus, Johnsons, Jeffreys, Hazlitts, or even M. de La Harpe, we glow with impatience at being always silent and itch to speak out and hail them as they pass, these newcomers, or else fire our whole artillery at them. Long ago Pindar said it about poems: Long live old wine and new ballads! New ballads—these may equally be this

1. In early 1857 the French government brought Flaubert to trial for the alleged immorality of his novel. He was acquitted.

evening's play or the latest novel, whatever is all the talk of young people at its first appearance.

I had not read *Madame Bovary* in its original form, in the periodical where the work was first published in successive chapters. However impressive the installments, something must have been lost in this process, which was bound above all to mar the overall thought and conception. Brought up short by scenes already daring in themselves, the reader wondered, "What will happen next?" It was possible to imagine the work taking the wildest directions and to suspect the author of intentions he never entertained. An uninterrupted reading puts each scene back into its true place. Before all else, *Madame Bovary* is a book, a book deliberately put together and planned, where everything coheres and nothing is left to chance, and in which the author, better say artist, has from start to finish done just what he wanted to do.

It is quite apparent that the author has spent much time in rural surroundings and in the Norman region which he describes with matchless fidelity. And here is something strange: when someone has lived a long time in the country, however deep his feeling for nature and however great his skill at depicting it, he has only a vague love for it; or at least he is most likely to represent it as beautiful only after he has left it. Then there is a tendency to set it in a frame of happiness, of felicity more or less fondly remembered, sometimes idyllic and wholly idealized. Bernardin de Saint-Pierre was thoroughly bored in Ile de France while he lived there, but once having returned, from afar off he was to think only of its beauty spots, the sweetness and peace of its valleys. In this setting he placed the creatures of his heart's desire: he wrote *Paul et Virginie*. Without going so far off as Bernardin de Saint-Pierre, Madame Sand, who had perhaps at first been bored in her native Berry, later delighted in representing it to us only in its rather attractive aspects. She did not disillusion us—far from it—about the banks of the Creuse; even while peopling the region with characters of intellect or passion, she admitted a liberal breath of the pastoral and rural, or the poetic as the ancients understood it. Here, with the author of *Madame Bovary*, we have to do with another procedure, with another mode of inspiration, and in fact with a different generation. The ideal has had its day; the lyrical is exhausted. We have gotten over them. A severe and pitiless truth, as the latest expression of experience, has penetrated even into art. Thus the author of *Madame Bovary* lived a provincial life, in the countryside and in market towns and hamlets. He didn't merely drive by on a spring day like La Bruyère's traveler,[2] who looking down from a hilltop conceives his own illusive scene, as though it were painted on the slope. He really lived there. And what did he see? Pettiness, wretchedness, pretense, stupidity, routine, monotony, and boredom—and he will say so. Those landscapes so truthfully and ingenuously depicted, breathing the rustic genius of the locale, he will use only as a setting for vulgar, dull creatures, for people absurdly ambitious, thoroughly ignorant or half-educated, for lovers devoid of delicacy. The single rare and pensive character who finds herself thrown into these surroundings, yearning for a world beyond, is out of her element, as it were, gasping for breath. Miserable, and lacking any kindred spirit in the place, she degenerates, becomes depraved, and in pursuit of empty dreams and absent charms arrives step by step at final perdition and ruin. Is this moral and comforting? The author seems not to have asked himself this question; he asked only, "Is it true?" We may suppose that he must actually have witnessed a situation like this, or at least delighted in condensing his various observations and their consequences into this closely unified picture, against a general background of bitterness and irony.

Here is another equally remarkable peculiarity: among all those very real and lifelike creatures, not one can be thought of as someone the author would like to be; none received his careful attention for any other purpose than to be described with unadorned precision; none has been humored as a friend is humored. He has held himself completely aloof; he is present only to see everything, to show everything, to tell everything. But nowhere in the novel do we glimpse so much as a shadow of the man himself. The work is entirely impersonal. This is a strong indication of power.

2. In his *Caractères*, La Bruyère tells of being charmed by the idyllic appearance of a small town seen on a clear day from high ground, which looked to him as if it were "painted on a hillside." He longed to spend his days in so delicious a spot, but a two-day sojourn among its inhabitants thoroughly disillusioned him.

Next to Madame Bovary, the most important character is M. Bovary. The younger Charles Bovary (he has a father of whom we are also given a lifelike portrayal) is revealed to us from his school days as a tidy boy, docile but awkward, a cipher or hopelessly mediocre, rather a blockhead, without the slightest distinction or initiative, dead to incentive, born to obey, to plod on in the beaten path and follow directions. Son of a former assistant surgeon-major, a rather disreputable person, he has nothing of either the daring or the vices of his father. His mother's thrift enabled him to pursue some paltry studies at Rouen, which led to his being licensed as a medical practitioner. The rank having been secured, not without difficulty, he has only to decide where to set up practice. He chooses Tostes, a little place not far from Dieppe; they marry him off to a widow much older than himself, who is said to have some income. To all this he offers no resistance, nor does it even occur to him that he is not happy.

One night he is unexpectedly summoned to a farm a good six leagues away to set a broken leg for old man Rouault, a widowed farmer who lives in easy circumstances with an only daughter. The nocturnal journey on horseback, the general setting and appearance of the rich farm, named Les Bertaux, Bovary's arrival and his welcome by the young girl, who is by no means a peasant type, having been educated as a young lady in a convent, the attitude of the patient—all this is admirably described, given us in careful detail as though we were seeing it in reality. It is a picture in the Dutch or Flemish manner, or rather the Norman. Bovary becomes accustomed to returning to Les Bertaux, and rather more often than is necessary for changing his patient's bandages. He continues to do so even after the cure is complete. Without his being aware of it his visits to the farm have gradually become a need, a delightful break in the routine of his laborious duties.

> On those days he got up early, set off at a gallop, urging on his horse; then he dismounted to wipe his shoes on the grass and put on his black gloves before entering the house. He liked making his arrival in the courtyard and noticing the gate yielding to the pressure of his shoulder, the rooster crowing on the wall, and the farm boys running to meet him. He liked the barn and the stables; he liked old

Rouault, who clasped his hand and called him his savior; he liked
Mlle Emma's small wooden shoes on the scrubbed flagstones of the
kitchen. Her heels made her slightly taller, and when she walked in
front of him her wooden soles, moving up and down, made a sharp
clatter against the leather of her shoes.

She always accompanied him to the bottom of the stairs. If they
had not yet fetched his horse, she would wait there. Having said their
good-bys, they would be silent; the breeze would swirl around her,
disheveling the light downy hair at the back of her neck, or flapping
her apron strings, which twisted like streamers against her hips. Once,
during a thaw, the bark of the trees in the yard was moist, and the
snow on the roofs of the buildings was melting. She stood on the
threshold; she went to fetch her umbrella; she opened it. The umbrella,
of translucent dove-colored silk, brightened the white skin of her face
with shifting hues. Beneath it she smiled in the gentle warmth, as the
drops of water were heard falling one by one on the taut silk.

Can there by any fresher or clearer picture than this, any more
sharply outlined or more luminous, any in which the reminiscence of
ancient form is better veiled in the modern manner? That sound of
melting snow dripping on the umbrella reminds me of another
sound made by fragments of ice tinkling as they fall from tree
branches onto the dry leaves of the path, in William Cowper's
"Winter Walk at Noon."[3] A rare excellence distinguishes M.
Gustave Flaubert from the other more or less accurate observers
who nowadays pride themselves on a conscientious rendition of
reality alone, and sometimes succeed: he has *style*. He even has
somewhat too much style, and his pen delights in curiosities and
*minutiae* of dramatic description which sometimes mar the total
effect. In his work the objects or characters most intended to engage
the reader's attention are somewhat blurred or flattened out by the
undue intrusion of surrounding objects. Madame Bovary, that
"Mademoiselle Emma" whom we have just seen so charming at her
first appearance, is so often described for us bit by bit, in minute
detail, that I retain no clear picture of her physical appearance as a
whole or in a very distinct and definite form.

3. A peculiarity of Sainte-Beuve's taste is the high value he assigned to what he
called the poetry of domestic life, a type epitomized for him in Cowper, to whom he
devoted a three-part *causerie* in 1854.

The first Madame Bovary dies and Mademoiselle Emma becomes the second and only Madame Bovary. The chapter on the wedding held at Les Bertaux is a perfect picture, of a rich and almost over-done truthfulness, a mingling of natural manners and Sunday-best finery, of ugliness, stiffness, coarse merriment and gracefulness, of revelry and delicate feeling. This wedding, the visit to the chateau La Vaubyessard and the ball there that form a kind of companion piece to the wedding itself, and the whole scene of the agricultural fair, introduced later on, make up pictures which, if they were done on canvas exactly as they are written, would deserve to hang in a gallery of the finest genre paintings.

So Emma becomes Madame Bovary, established in the little house at Tostes, in cramped quarters, with a tiny garden longer than it is wide and open to the fields beyond. She soon makes everything orderly, neat, and elegant. Her husband, who thinks only of pleasing her, buys a carriage, a secondhand buggy, so that whenever she wishes she can take a drive along the high road or around the neighborhood. For the first time in his life he feels himself to be a happy man; busy all day with his patients, he returns home to a sense of joy and delicious intoxication; he is in love with his wife. He asks no more than that this peaceful domestic contentment should endure. But his wife, who has dreamed of better things and had often wondered in the boring hours of her girlhood how to find happiness, quite soon becomes aware, even during their honeymoon, that she is not happy.

At this point begins a close, probing, delicate analysis, the first incision of a cruel dissection which will continue to the end of the book. We enter into the very heart of Madame Bovary. How define that heart?—she is a woman, and at first only romantic, not at all corrupt. Her portrayer, M. Gustave Flaubert, does not spare her. By denouncing even the coquettish and finicky tastes she had as a little girl at boarding school, by picturing her as a daydreamer with an oversensitive imagination, he exposes her without mercy; and —dare I confess it?—on careful reflection the reader is more indul-gent to her than the author seems to be. In the situation in which she finds herself from now on, and to which she must become accustomed, Emma has one quality in excess, or one virtue too few:

herein lies the source of her mistakes and misfortunes. The quality in excess is a temperament not only romantic but beset with needs of the heart, of intelligence and ambition, a temperament aspiring to a loftier, more select, and more elegant life than the one that has fallen to her lot. The missing virtue is never having learned that the first requirement for successful living is a capacity to put up with boredom, with the vague sense of having missed out on a life more agreeable and more in conformity with our tastes. She is unable to submit silently and hide her feelings, to create a role for herself, whether in the love of her child or in being of use to those around her—any useful activity, attachment, or salutary goal. To be sure, she struggles; she does not stray from the straight path in a day. She will have to make many attempts over several years before plunging into wrongdoing. Each day, however, she takes one step closer until at last she is astray beyond redemption. But I am analyzing, whereas the author of *Madame Bovary* aimed only to let us see his heroine day by day, minute by minute, in thought and action.

The long, sad days of the lovely Emma, left to herself in the first months of marriage, her walks to the beech grove at Banneville with Djali, her faithful greyhound, while she questions herself about destiny and wonders what "might have been"—all this is unraveled and set forth with the same analytical finesse and delicacy as in the most intimately personal novel of yesteryear designed to nourish our romantic dreams. Impressions of rustic nature, as in the period of René or Obermann,[4] fitfully and capriciously mingle themselves with the spiritual boredom, stirring vague desires:

Sometimes there were gusts of wind, sea breezes that suddenly swept over the whole plateau around Caux, carrying their salty freshness to the distant fields. Bent close to the ground, the reeds whistled, and the shivering leaves of the beech trees rustled, while their ever swaying tops kept up a great murmuring. Emma drew her shawl closer about her shoulders and stood up.

Along the tree-lined way a green light dimmed by the foliage shone on the smooth moss that crunched softly beneath her feet. The sun was setting; the sky was red between the branches, and the identical tree

4. Etienne Pinert de Sénancour's *Obermann* (1804), expressive like Chateaubriand's *René* of romantic melancholy, was edited by Sainte-Beuve in 1833.

trunks planted in a straight line looked like brown columns against a
golden background. A wave of fear gripped her. She called to Djali,
returned quickly to Tostes by the main road, sank into an armchair,
and never uttered a word all evening.

At about this time a neighbor, the Marquis d'Andervilliers, who
was about to run for office, gives a great ball at the chateau, to
which he invites all the notable and influential people of the district.
It was by mere chance that he had met Bovary, who in the absence
of any other doctor one day treated him for an abscess of the mouth.
On a visit to Tostes, the marquis had had a single glimpse of
Madame Bovary and on the spot judged her sufficiently proper to
be invited to the ball. Hence the visit of M. and Mme Bovary to the
chateau La Vaubyessard. This is one of the most important and
most deftly handled parts of the book.

That evening affair, where Emma is received with the courtesy
everywhere shown to a pretty young woman, where she inhales that
perfume of elegant, aristocratic living she dreams of and thinks
herself born for, where she dances, waltzes without ever having
learned how, where she instinctively does everything that the
occasion requires—that affair where she succeeds so nicely will completely go to her head and contribute to her ruin: she poisons herself, so to speak, in its fragrance. Only very slowly will the poison
take effect, but she will never again get it out of her blood. Every
incident, even the most trifling, of that single memorable evening
remains engraved in her heart, where it will do its secret work.
"Her trip to La Vaubyessard had made a gap in her life like one of
those huge crevasses that a storm sometimes excavates overnight in
a mountain." When on the day after the ball, having left La
Vaubyessard in the morning and gotten back at dinner time, M.
and Mme Bovary found themselves once again in their little home
seated at their modest table graced with hot onion soup and a platter
of veal and sorrel, Bovary rubs his hands and says, "How good it is
to be home again!" She looks at him with unspeakable contempt.
Her own spirit has traveled a great distance since the previous day,
and in an entirely opposite direction. When the two of them set out
in their buggy for the party they were only two quite different
people; after their return an abyss has opened between them.

What I have summarized here fills pages and extends over years. To be fair to Emma, she does take her time about it. In her effort to be prudent she seeks auxiliaries both within herself and about her. Within herself she has a serious deficiency: she lacks courage; her imagination has long since absorbed all else. And about her—once again she is unlucky: this poor Charles who loves her, and whom at times she has made an effort to love, lacks the intelligence to understand her, to divine her nature. If he were at least ambitious, if he cared about distinguishing himself in his profession, bettering himself by study and work, making his name known and respected. But no: he has neither ambition nor curiosity, not a single one of the drives that urge a man to get out of his ambit and move ahead, and that make a wife proud to have people know she bears his name. She is incensed by it. "Why, he's not a man. What a wretched man!" she exclaims, "what a wretched man!" Once humiliated by him, she will never forgive him.

At last she becomes afflicted with the kind of disease they call a nervous ailment, a sort of nostalgia, a homesickness for a land unknown. Ever blind and ever devoted, Charles tries everything to cure her, and unable to think of anything better than a change of air therefore leaves Tostes and his growing practice to establish himself in another corner of Normandy, in the *arrondissement* of Neufchâtel, in a bustling town named Yonville-l'Abbaye. Up to this point the novel has only had its prelude: not until after they are settled at Yonville does the plot really begin, and the action, allowing always for painstaking analytical comment, move at a faster pace.

At the time of this change of location, Madame Bovary is pregnant with her first and only child, a daughter. This child will act as a slight counterweight in her life, slowing down her drift toward evil by an access, no more than a whim really, of affection. However, her maternal feelings are ill prepared; her breast is already too filled with barren passions and sterile ambitions to accommodate the sort of natural affections that demand personal sacrifice.

The new region where they settle, bordering on Picardy, "a degenerate country where the speech is without accent and the landscape without character," is described with unsparing truthfulness. The town and its principal inhabitants, the vicar, the tax collector, the innkeeper, the sexton, the notary, etc., are drawn straight from life, unforgettably. Among the characters now introduced and destined, officious busybodies as they are, to be with us to the end, the pharmacist M. Homais stands out in boldest relief, a creation of M. Flaubert who rises to the level of a type. We have all met M. Homais before, but never in so florid and triumphant a guise: he is the town's man of importance, mouthing commonplaces, a braggart who fancies himself above prejudice, banal and affected, artful and scheming, knowing in his very stupidity. M. Homais is the Prudhomme[5] of half-knowledge.

The Bovarys become acquainted with some of the leading personages of the place on their first day there, when they stop at the Golden Lion. But among the other frequenters of the inn there is M. Léon Dupuis, who makes a special point of conversing with Madame Bovary at table. And immediately, in admirably managed dialogue, thoroughly lifelike and ironic, the author shows us the two of them mutually attracted by what is least genuine in them, their taste for the vaguely poetic and romantic, the whole procedure a mask for mischief. Though only a beginning, it has something about it disconcerting to those who believe in poetry of the heart and indulge in sentimental elegy. Clearly their behavior is known, aped, and parodied; it's enough to spoil one's taste for dialogues of love seriously intended.

Events are not to transpire as you might imagine. This little M. Léon will gain ground in Madame Bovary's affections, but not right away, not yet. For some time Madame Bovary is outwardly an honest woman, though her secret name, already lightly inscribed, be *Treachery* or *Faithlessness*. At bottom this M. Léon doesn't amount to much; still, he's young, he seems goodhearted, and he thinks he's in love. This situation is both sustained and suspended by the constraints of an existence so constantly observed by others that they could hardly meet, as well as by their shyness toward each other. She struggles within herself, although no one gives her credit for it. "What exasperated her was that her husband gave no sign of

5. A reference to M. Joseph Prudhomme, a creation of the French caricaturist Henri Monnier (1799–1877), representing the type of the prosperous and platitudinous bourgeois.

suspecting her torment." One day she tries to bare her soul to the good vicar, M. Bournisien, a vulgar, dull-spirited person who hasn't the remotest notion of what her moral problem is. Fortunately, while all this is going on, the time comes for Léon to leave for Paris to continue his study of the law. Their constrained farewells, the suppressed grief, the various hints of what they secretly take to be hopelessness, her yearning for him, magnified afterwards in memory aided by imagination, are all subjected to a perfectly coherent, penetrating analysis with a continuous underlying irony.

The great day of the year for Yonville l'Abbaye is when they hold the Seine-Inférieure agricultural show there. The depiction of this celebrated day's events constitutes the third great set piece of the book; it is a masterpiece in its kind. There Madame Bovary's fate is decided. A handsome gentleman of the neighborhood, M. Rodolphe Boulanger de la Huchette, had seen her a few days before when he brought a peasant to her husband to be bled. This M. Rodolphe, thirty-four years old, coarse but superficially elegant, a great ladies' man with a natural weakness for skirt chasing, noted that Madame Bovary had remarkably pretty eyes and would suit him very nicely. On the day of the famous fair he never leaves her side; although he is a member of the judges' panel, he gives up his official place on the platform to be with her. And now occurs a delicious, well-wrought scene: while the presiding councilor of the prefecture dilates in the gravest tones upon the economic, industrial, political, and moral considerations appropriate to the occasion, Rodolphe, at a window of the town hall, whispers into Madame Bovary's ear the timeworn phrases that have so often served his turn with other daughters of Eve. That solemn official oration, so full of bombast, intermittently broken into by the equally trite sentimental cooings of this tender declaration, is a highly effective piece of sustained irony. The result is predictable! Madame Bovary, whose heart had been shaken by Léon and who regretted having resisted him so strongly, will quickly yield to this newcomer, who in his fatuity will take exclusive credit for his success. All these caprices and inconsistencies of female psychology are accurately observed.

Having once taken the first decisive step, Madame Bovary moves quickly to make up for lost time. Madly in love with Rodolphe, she throws herself at him with no fear of compromising herself for his sake. From now on we shall follow her at greater distance. The episode of the clubfoot, a botched operation performed by her husband, puts a final end to whatever affection and respect she had ever felt for him. In her frenzied passion she reaches the point of being no longer able to bear Rodolphe's absence for a single day and beseeches him to carry her off to a cottage in the depths of the forest or a cabin by the sea. One scene is especially moving and poignant. Back one night from his daily rounds, Bovary (who, poor fellow, suspects nothing) falls to dreaming at his daughter's cradle of all the good things he plans for the child, for his little Bertha's future. Lying near him, feigning sleep, his wife for her part dreams only of the next morning's abduction in a post chaise drawn by four horses, of romantic delights, imaginary voyages, the Orient, Granada, the Alhambra, and suchlike. These simultaneous but utterly contrasting reveries, of the wronged father envisaging only the pure delights of domestic bliss and of the beautiful and passionate adulteress who wants to smash it all to pieces, are the work of an artist who, having once grasped his theme, knows how to make the most of it.

Some expressions taken straight from life are worth special notice. One evening when Rodolphe, on a visit to Madame Bovary, is seated in the consulting room at an hour when no one was ever there, they hear a noise. "Do you have your pistols?" Emma asks. Her words make him laugh. Against whom would he have to use pistols except her own husband, whom he has not the slightest desire to kill? All the same, the words were spoken. Madame Bovary had doubtless uttered them without thinking; nonetheless, she is one of those women who, pressed by necessity and the rage of passion, would stop at nothing. She will prove this again later when on a trip to Rouen, after being abandoned by Rodolphe (who is willing enough to enjoy a pretty neighbor but does not at all care for abducting her), she comes on Léon, now depraved and no longer timid. She herself has given way to ignoble impulses, wrecked her home life, and contracted debts unknown to her husband. One day, no longer knowing where to turn and threatened by the law, she asks Léon to get her 3,000 francs immediately. She says to him,

"If I were in your place I'd know where to find them." "Where?" "In your law office." Clearly, Madame Bovary would go to the length of inciting her lovers to murder, had they been capable of it, and even to the final degradation of theft. But it is well that the reader is given no glimpse of these frightful possibilities except by some piercing words spoken on a single occasion.

In the latter half of the book, which is written with no less diligence and precision than the first, I should like to mention one flaw that becomes unduly noticeable. Without the author's having intended it, but simply as a result of his method of describing everything and leaving nothing out of account, there are some vividly indelicate details that come very close to sensual incitement. Certainly he ought not to have gone this far. After all, a book is not and never could be reality itself. Carried beyond a certain point, description defeats the purpose—I will not say of the moralist—but of every scrupulous artist. It is true that except in the most risqué and daring passages M. Flaubert's attitude remains highly bitter and ironic; his tone is never one of indulgence or complicity; in the last analysis nothing could be less alluring. But he should consider that some French readers are of that malicious turn of mind that imputes evil intent wherever it can do so.

Madame Bovary's frightful end, her punishment if you will, her death, is set forth in pitiless detail. The author does not shrink from dwelling on this harsh strain until it grates on our nerves. Bovary's death, which occurs soon after, is very moving and gains our sympathy for this poor good man. I have mentioned the inadvertent natural expressions that are so frighteningly realistic. In his grief over the loss of his wife, to whose offenses he has remained as blind as possible, Bovary still relates everything to her. On receiving an invitation to Léon's wedding, he exclaims, "How happy this would have made my poor wife!" Shortly thereafter, when he has discovered the bundle of letters from both Léon and Rodolphe, he forgives everything. Still in love with the worthless and ungrateful woman he has lost, he dies of grief.

At certain moments of the story it would have been easy to add a touch of the ideal to the reality, to round out and, as it were, redeem the character. Take Charles Bovary at the end, for example:

had the sculptor wished it, a light touch of his thumb to the clay he was molding would have sufficed to convert instantly a vulgar likeness into a noble and affecting figure. The reader would have been well disposed toward this, indeed almost demands it. But the author consistently refuses, having determined against it.

Right after the burial of his daughter, old father Rouault, though overcome with grief, utters a typically peasantlike expression that is ludicrous and yet sublimely natural. Each year he has sent Charles Bovary a turkey in remembrance of the setting of his broken leg; now as he takes his tearful leave he speaks a final word of tender feeling: "Don't worry, you'll still receive your turkey."

While making full allowance for the deliberate bias which is inherent in the author's very method and which constitutes his "poetic," one objection I have to his book is that it is too lacking in the quality of goodness; not one character represents this quality. The sole devoted, disinterested person, who never dared tell his love, M. Homais's little apprentice Justin, is negligible. Why wasn't there a single figure calculated to console the reader, to refresh him by some display of goodness? Why could he not have been spared one friend? Why justify the reproach: "Moralist, you understand everything, but you are cruel"? To be sure, the book has its moral. The author has not stated it in so many words; it is up to the reader to infer it, and a frightening one it is too. But is it the duty of art to refuse to console, to eschew any element of mercy or good nature, on the pretext of being truthful? Besides, truth, even if that is the only aim, is not entirely and necessarily on the side of evil, of human stupidity and perversity. In this provincial life, so replete with bickering and persecutions, with paltry aspirations and petty slanders, there are also fine, decent souls, who have remained inoffensive and kept themselves freer of worldliness than is the case elsewhere. There is modesty, submissiveness, self-sacrifice over long years; who among us cannot mention examples? In spite of yourself, even in your very lifelike characters you do rather load the dice and skillfully combine eccentricities and absurdities. Why not also show some good qualities united in at least one attractive and estimable figure? I knew a young woman of superior intelligence and ardent spirit, who was suffering boredom far off in a province of central France. Married, but with no child to rear and love, what did she do to put her abundant spiritual energy to use? She adopted the children living around her. She set herself to become an active benefactress, a civilizing force in the rather wild country in which fate had placed her. She gave reading lessons and moral instruction to the children of the villagers, many of whom lived a good distance away and widely scattered. She sometimes voluntarily traveled a league and a half on foot, her pupil meeting her halfway, and the lesson was given in a footpath, under a tree, or on a heath. There are souls of this kind to be found in the provinces and out in the country. Why not show them as well? That would raise our spirits, console us, and provide a more complete picture of humanity.

These are my objections to a book whose merits, accuracy of observation, style (save a few blemishes), design, and composition, I rate very highly.

On the whole, the work bears the stamp of its time. Begun, as I understand, several years ago, its publication at this moment is timely. It is indeed a suitable book to read after listening to the plain, steely dialogue of a comedy by Alexandre Dumas the younger, or applauding *Les Faux Bonhommes*, between the perusal of a couple of Taine's essays. For in many places, and in diverse forms, I think I can recognize certain new literary symptoms: science, a spirit of observation, maturity, power, a slight toughness. These are the traits which the leaders of the new generation seem to affect. Son and brother of distinguished physicians, M. Gustave Flaubert handles the pen as others handle the scalpel. Anatomists and physiologists, I find you everywhere!

*Causeries du lundi*, XIII, 346–63 (May 4, 1857).

# Virgil and the Epic

*Sainte-Beuve was not, and made no pretense of being, a professional clas-*
*sicist. He knew and loved Greek and Roman literature and kept himself*
*informed of new developments in classical scholarship. But Sainte-Beuve's*
*antiquity is the antiquity of the humanist, for whom Homer and Virgil and*
*their literary countrymen are less objects of historical speculation or philological*
*research than the first and purest embodiments of a still living cultural*
*tradition. If the* Aeneid *is, as Sainte-Beuve insists, peculiarly expressive of*
*its own time and place, Virgil is also, in an order of literature that transcends*
*the categories of past and present, "the first of the Racinian poets."*

## 1. AN EPIC POET WRITES OF HIS OWN TIME

\* \* \* There has been much discussion of a question which
arises most appropriately [in reference to Virgil]. Again quite
recently an English author, Mr. Matthew Arnold, son of a respected
and celebrated father and quite distinguished in his own right, in
the preface to a collection of his poems (1853) asked himself whether,
from the standpoint of classical art and beauty, it was not better for
a poet aspiring to lofty and austere poetry to choose subjects from
the past, even the remotest past, provided only that they be subjects
in which he can find ready to hand the principal constituents and
eternal passions of human nature. Mr. Arnold has ably evinced the
inexhaustible interest which adheres and will forever adhere to the
*Iliad*, to Sophocles' *Electra*, to that trilogy of Aeschylus which goes
by the name of the *Oresteia*, and to the episode of Dido [in the *Aeneid*],
and he contrasts it with the interest which adorns those modern
poems that are more or less related to romance, such as [Goethe's]
*Hermann und Dorothea* for example, or *Childe Harold*, or Wordsworth's

*Excursion*, or even the delightful *Jocelyn*.[1] He further wondered
whether the great public subjects of modern times were as propitious for poetry as the ancient, whether we were not living today
in times that are above all too "enlightened," in which present
events become almost incapable of poetic treatment and belong by
right only to the historian. He pointed out that Aeschylus's *The
Persians* had never been reputed superior in interest to his other
tragedies. This is all quite true, and by arguing in this fashion the
ingenious English author has shown himself to be a true classical
critic of the school of Lessing. Nevertheless, in these questions,
which criticism disputes in vain and only natural talent can decide
or solve, there is one point which I will always insist upon: it is
important and necessary that a poem have life—a life real in its
time for the poet's contemporaries, not a cold life meaningful only
to a few connoisseurs in their studies—that it have a modern
element, an interest up-to-date and recent, even though it is adapted
to an ancient subject and, as it were, infused into it. And to begin
with (since we are speaking of the classics) I have Homer on my
side. In the very first book of the *Odyssey* Phemius is present at the
feast of the suitors, singing the woes of the Trojan War and the
mishaps of the homeward journey. Secluded in her private quarters,
Penelope hears him; she comes down to the hall and bids him
perform as many poetic recitals of the other deeds of men and gods
as he knows, but to forego the recent and distressing theme which
awakens all her conjugal grief. At this, Telemachus becomes almost
angry and takes the bard's part. "My mother, why do you reproach
the melodious bard for singing to us just as his thoughts prompt and
inspire him to do? The bards are not to blame, but only Jupiter,
who accords to each man what fortune he pleases. There is no call
to be angered at this man for singing the evil destiny of the Greeks;
*for the song men most applaud is the newest and latest they have heard.*"
This is the novelty which writers must know how to instill into
every masterpiece, in a manner appropriate to it, joining the new
with the lasting conditions of things. Without this newness there can
be no emotion or excitement, no poetic ardor.

1. The first part of a long "metaphysical epic" which Lamartine published in
1836.

Virgil knew how to achieve it more than any other epic poet since Homer. What a great many of those cyclic, epic poets there had been in Greece since Homer! how many talented men whose works have perished and whose very names we hardly know—an Arctinus, a Lesches, a Pisander, a Panyasis, Herodotus's uncle, an Antimachus—all of them names once celebrated in the train of Homer![2] As early as the Peloponnesian War, Choerilus complained of having arrived too late, when the "meadows of the Muses" had been completely reaped and despoiled of their flowers.[3] Virgil, though a Roman and more at ease because of the greater lapse of time, nonetheless came after so many others before him, predecessors whose names are lost to us, that he felt the same embarrassment. With both concern and an awareness of his own powers, he gave it expression at the beginning of the third book of the *Georgics*: "Every subject"—he means especially every Greek subject—"has already been exhausted and worn out. . . . I must attempt a new way by which I too may rise aloft and soar victoriously from tongue to tongue in men's report." To what lengths, accordingly, did he not go in order to overcome the commonplace in the epic and rejuvenate its poetic theme? First of all he had the skill to unite Roman pride and patriotic feeling, with all their ardent ambitions, to that celebration of Aeneas and the oft-told tale of the sufferings and calamities of Troy. At the very heart of his composition, whether by means of Aeneas's miraculous shield or in the Pythagorian perspectives of his Elysium and Anchises' prophecies, he displayed the whole history of the grandeur and future eternity of Rome.[4] He showed even the moment of crisis in that grandeur and the terrible

2. Arctinus of Miletus, author of an *Aethiopis*, Lesches of Lesbos, reputed author of a "Little Iliad," and Antimachus, reputed author of an *Epigoni*, belong to the so-called epic cycle. Only a few lines of these vast works are extant. Peisander of Rhodes and Panyasis of Halicarnassus both wrote epics on Hercules during the seventh and fifth centuries B.C., respectively.

3. Presumably Choerilus of Samos, a friend of the historian Herodotus (fifth century B.C.). A few fragments of his epic *Perseis* remain, including the opening lines containing the complaint to which Sainte-Beuve here alludes.

4. During his visit to the underworld in the sixth book of the *Aeneid*, Aeneas meets in the Elysian Fields the shade of his father, Anchises, who predicts the future glories of the Rome his son is destined to found.

dangers incurred, when he has his Dido, from atop her pyre, foretell the coming of Hannibal. * * *

With a natural and happy incoherence, Anchises thus constantly departs from chronological sequence [in his prophecy] to follow the lead of his heart, that is to say, the feelings that were alive at the time when Virgil was writing * * * . He sums up the entire spirit of his prophetic history in that famous and magnificent definition of the unique virtue and excellence of Rome: "To other nations be the triumphs of art, the wonders of statuary, even the science of the heavens. Be it yours, O Romans, to govern the peoples, to decree peace or war, to spare the vanquished and war down the haughty; yours to be the nation preeminent in the arts of practical politics, the royal race." [5]

I have rendered only the gist of this immortal passage, in which old Anchises promulgated the magnificent theme upon which all the Machiavellis and Montesquieus would afterwards have only to expand and subsist. [6]

## 2. HOMER THE EPIC BARD, VIRGIL THE EPIC POET

Setting aside the general definitions of what constitutes an epic poem or an epic tale (because these things are always better grasped by reading the poets than through abstract formulas) I cannot, however, avoid laying down the broad distinction between the types.

There was the primitive epic tale, the Homeric *rhapsody*, what in the Middle Ages was called the *chanson de geste*, a type of story recited publicly, often accompanied by music (of a very somber strain), in what amounted to a kind of clearly articulated and accented recitative. And then there was and still is the epic poem properly so called, a work of deep private meditation, the noblest of poetic creations, produced in eras of culture and refined taste.

With the two poems ascribed to him—and in their overall structure they really do seem to bear the imprint of a single genius—

5. *Aeneid* 6, lines 847–53.

6. Machiavelli's *Discorsi* and Montesquieu's *Grandeur et décadence des Romaines* laud ancient Rome.

Homer offers the greatest and finest example of the first species of epic narration, at a time when the poet was truly a *bard*. He is the father and god (so to speak) of that pristine race of divine bards whom he himself introduced as characters in his poems, forerunners of the Homerides,[7] Phemius at Ithaca and Demodocus among the Phaeacians. They are old men, blind, persons of honor, who perform at assemblies and banquets and know an assortment of stories about men and gods, but especially about recent great events, which excite the curiosity and stir the imagination of their contemporaries. There is no simpler or more pleasant way to describe them than to borrow Homer's own words. At the palace of Alcinoüs, Ulysses sees Demodocus appear in the midst of the banquet. He has the herald take him a choice slice of boar's meat, a serving of honor. "Herald," he says, "take this meat to Demodocus and tell him I give him greeting, afflicted though I be; for, among all men inhabiting the earth, the bards have received honor and respect as their portion, because the Muse has taught them harmonious song and cherished the race of bards." And he addresses him: "O Demodocus, I glorify you above all mortals. Either the Muse, daughter of Jupiter, or Apollo himself has taught you; for in admirable order you sing the calamity of the Greeks, what they did and suffered, and all the labors they endured, as though you yourself had been there or had heard it from another who was." Indeed, one of the peculiar marks of that ancient race of poets is that they derive their songs from close to the source, and so create in their audience the illusion of either having themselves seen the events they celebrate or else having been informed by other eyewitnesses: *reality* lives in their songs. Continuing his remarks, Ulysses then asks Demodocus to recite him the particular episode of the wooden horse, that stratagem devised by Ulysses himself for the destruction of Troy. "If you can fittingly recite that whole story to me, I in turn will be eager to tell all men that a benevolent god has given you the divine gift of song."[8]

Praise and renown, in fact, are what the bard regards as the

7. These were the rhapsodists who spread Homer's fame throughout Greece by reciting his epics.

8. *Odyssey* 8, lines 477–81, 487–98.

greatest compensation, and Ulysses knows how to win his favor by a commendation that delights his heart. This love of glory remained a distinctive trait of the Greeks. Horace in his time recognized this fact about them; glory was their one ambition, their only "avarice"; they were "covetous of honor" and of nothing else, in contrast to the Romans, a practical people who by virtue of sound institutions certainly did attain to the proud worship of high renown but were soon afflicted with the blight of usury and a concern for lucre. "And it was in this love of glory, the spur to every great enterprise," Xenophon tells us, "that the Athenians surpassed all the other Greeks, much more than in the euphony of their speech or in any particular bodily virtue or excellence."[9]

It has been thought that in the praises spoken by Ulysses Homer gives an indirect portrayal of himself in the person of Demodocus. "He put himself into his poem," says Eustathius;[10] at the very least we may assume that he mirrored himself unconsciously.

I have hardly touched upon the passages which afford us a picture of that liberal, honored, prosperous estate which the bards enjoyed among the ancient Greeks. They were an essential part of the social life and of festive gatherings. "For I maintain"—once again it is Ulysses speaking at Alcinoüs's table—"that there is no more gracious occasion in life than when joy possesses a whole people, and the feasters, seated in order in the hall, are listening to a bard, while the tables are laden with bread and meat, and the cupbearer, drawing wine into the decanter, carries it around the board, filling each cup in turn; to me, there is nothing finer than this."[11] It was the poet Gray, I believe, who said that for him paradise consisted in reclining on a sofa reading a good novel. I think we can even now call up an image of this refined and sensitive reader secluded on a summer's day behind drawn blinds in a quiet meditative chamber. Here we have the other extreme, which characterizes the highly civilized literary life. In sharp contrast to this, the primitive pleasure of the Greeks described by Ulysses is social, one that assigns poetry a far

9. I cannot discover the exact source of this quotation from Xenophon.

10. The twelfth-century Byzantine scholar Eustathius wrote valuable commentaries on Homer.

11. *Odyssey* 9, lines 5–11.

ampler and nobler role in the mainstream of the community's life and customs. Those times were truly the heyday of the lyre, "which the gods made the consort of feasts."

Here in the *Odyssey*, then, in this naive representation, we have a picture of the early epic singers, those men of vast memories, who could at will recall any particular passage or episode suggested by the inspiration of the moment or called for by the master of the house. Among a people enamored of song and glory these men held exalted rank and enjoyed an almost priestly dignity. In their recital the most painful misfortunes and calamities became pleasurable, and it seemed that men could never reward them too much, since by doing so they would gain the honor of diverting and delighting posterity. "It is the gods who have willed it so," Alcinoüs tells Ulysses, in tears at the recital of his own sufferings, "and they have visited these calamities upon men in order that they might thereafter become the subject of song, even for nations yet to be." [12] Here again we meet the Greek idea of glory, the grand consummation that makes amends for all else!

Now it is obvious that the chief function of this tribe of bards was to hold their hearers' interest and give them delight; what moral instruction they contrived to mingle in their songs occupied only a secondary place. Poets, Horace tells us, aim to instruct or to please, or to do both at once; to utter delightful words which also prove to be applicable to life. Homer's undying distinction lies in having united, in the vast and sublime collections which comprise his poems, the highest degree of pleasure and the liveliest power with an inner and unconscious morality, the kind that emerges and overflows from the work without deliberate intention, in a sort of natural outpouring. Homer may be likened to the great rivers which we see represented in our gardens by statues of old men; he carelessly tips the urn brimful of moralities and out they pour.

With Virgil the procedure is entirely different. But how many centuries had rolled by between him and Homer, a thousand years perhaps! What vast changes in manners and customs had in the meantime occurred! The art of writing had settled the poetic texts, and professional critics had necessarily left their mark on them as

12. *Odyssey* 8, lines 579–80.

soon as they passed from oral to written form. The Homerides, those
direct disciples of Homer, plus a long series of epic and cyclic poets,
had imitated the great legendary bard, scrupulously following his
example and forming themselves on his model; learned schools had
been cultivating the epic as a genre of literature; capping the whole
was Aristotle, the intellectual legislator of antiquity, who came to
fix the limits and establish the laws and principles of the several
orders of literary composition. Virgil, born in a country whose
literature had originally been borrowed and transplanted from
Greece, found himself, more than anyone else if possible, under the
influence of these cultural conditions and thus subjected to all the
rules and conventions of the secondary epic. I submit, however, that
the very differences between the epic tale as it was performed and
solemnized in Homer's time and what it was conceived to be in the
age of Virgil were entirely congenial to the Roman poet's peculiar
talent and far more calculated to sustain and aid than to frustrate
and restrict him. For just as Homer was the grand prototype of
those aged blind singers who, lyre in hand, sang their tales at public
assemblies and banquets, men whom the listening throng inspired
and in whose creations the line between improvisation and composition is blurred by a wizardlike memory, so Virgil is and will
forever remain the chief of poets who compose in the privacy of
their rooms, who study long and meditate, who revise constantly
and improvise never. He himself is said to have compared the
products of his pen to bear cubs, which are born ugly and lumpish
and have to be licked into form and shapeliness by their mothers.
After a burst of composition during the forenoon, he would spend
the rest of the day in revising and improving his verses. Meticulous
and correct, he observes every nicety, leaving nothing to chance;
this was Virgil's own peculiar means of calling into play his full
creative vein. He is one of those poets who take the precaution of
roughing out their poems in prose before turning them into verse,
as is said to have been his practice in composing the *Aeneid*. He is
one of those whom the crowd does not inspire but intimidates, and
the story goes that whenever he became aware of being recognized
and followed in the streets of Rome, which he seldom visited, he
would quickly disappear into the first house he came to. Virgil was

not the man to fill a vast banquet hall with the sound of his voice, preferring instead to read to a small gathering of friends. In short, in the whole tenor of his personality and artistic manner Virgil is, for the epic, the first of the Racinian poets (if I may be allowed an anachronism that conveys my thought in a single word), the fullest and most perfect example of the type.[13] He stands at the head, or, as Montaigne would say, is the chorus leader, of the second group, as against the group headed by Homer. For Virgil, the stricter literary laws, including the epic rules themselves, were no hindrance but rather a source of strength and beauty.

As to the character of his epic narration, defining it only by those general features he still shares with Homer but to which he gave a greater polish and clarity, I should say that the epic poem as Virgil understood it is an austere, elevated, ornate, grave, moving narration, designed to elicit both admiration and delight and to stir the noblest powers of the soul. It is a poetry wedded to history, and to an affection for religion, country, humanity, and family, to ancestral piety and regard for posterity, to every grand and virtuous feeling as well as to delicate and tender sentiment without effeminacy, pathos tempered with decency; a magnificent poetry yielding indirect and salutary instruction derived from deeply felt impressions set forth in beautiful lines which engrave themselves upon the reader's consciousness; a poetry which, to indicate its quality by its most illustrious readers, found a place in the treasure casket of an Augustus, or on the bed table of a Chatham, a Fox, or a Fénelon (under which name I would designate every man of good taste and feeling). Such then is the regular epic, no longer Homeric but belonging to the later period of antiquity and already modern—as it may be generally defined from a reading of Virgil and in its most favorable acceptation.

*Etude sur Virgile*, pp. 72–75, 77–78, 83–90 (1857).

13. Another example of Sainte-Beuve's "families of minds."

# Alexander Pope

*To Hippolyte Adolphe Taine's epoch-making* Histoire de la littérature anglaise (1864) *Sainte-Beuve devoted a review comprising three consecutive* Lundis. *He expressed considerable approval of this new mode of literary history, according to which Taine discussed English literature as so many products of the three conditioning forces of the race, the milieu, and the moment, although Sainte-Beuve easily detects its crippling neglect of an indispensable and unpredictable fourth force: the individual talent. But for English readers the most arresting portion of this famous review is the appraisal of Alexander Pope, which Sainte-Beuve included as a corrective to the largely unfavorable account given in Taine's third volume. If Taine could not admire Pope's art, neither, with rare exceptions, could Pope's own nineteenth-century countrymen. Sainte-Beuve's highly sympathetic treatment is therefore eloquent demonstration of how far his appreciative capacities transcended the usual limits of romantic-Victorian taste.*

\* \* \* After Milton, the many-sided, fertile, pliable, uneven Dryden, the transitional figure and in order of time the first of the classics but still broad and powerful, has little to complain of at M. Taine's hands: the critic gives us a good explanation of that checkered and care-ridden life and of that talent which, like his career, was somewhat governed by chance and yet ample, abundant, imaginative, vigorous, and fed and watered by a copious poetic vein.

It is rather the great poet of the following age, Pope, the classical poet in the perfection of correctness and concise elegance, who has no reason to be pleased by M. Taine; and since to avoid monotony praise must be varied by some caviling, I shall take the liberty of contradicting him a little on this matter.

139

Not that elegance and politeness as such in the person and talent of Pope displease M. Taine, for no one has a better appreciation than he of Addison, the first model of English urbanity, insofar as it exists. He makes an excellent judgment of Addison's moderate, discreet, moral, decorous manner, that *Quod decet* [that which is seemly] which he was the first to teach his countrymen. He does full justice to the various characters so ably sketched in the *Spectator*, whose aspect is always so typically English. But when it comes to Pope, M. Taine fails to make that effort which on occasion a literary historian finds it necessary to exert over himself and even against himself, and so he introduces to us with marked disfavor and disapproval the poet so long esteemed the most perfect of his nation and proclaimed as such again by Byron.

Nothing is easier than to make a caricature of Pope, but nothing is more unjust to great minds than to dwell exclusively on their failings and on the weak or petty facets of their natures. Must we first and foremost see in Pope only "a dwarf, four feet tall, contorted, hunchbacked, thin, valetudinarian, appearing, when he reached maturity, no longer capable of existing"? Is it fitting immediately to take advantage of his bodily infirmities, as against his charming wit, by telling us: "He could not get up by himself, a woman dressed him; he wore three pairs of stockings, drawn on one over the other, so slender were his legs; then he was laced up in a corset of stiff canvas, so that he could hold himself erect, over which he wore a flannel waistcoat . . ."? I am hardly the one to blame a critic for calling attention, even in detail, to his author's physiology or telling us how good or bad his health was, things that certainly influence his intellectual character and talent; the point is, however, that Pope did not write with his muscles but only with his mind. In M. Taine's description (which I quoted only in part) I am shocked only by his choice of words and the harsh and unkind manner in which Pope is treated, tending to make him ridiculous in the reader's mind. Let us leave this kind of thing to those whose only aim in writing is to amuse or else heedlessly to give rein to their aversions. If one had known Horace, I suppose it would have been possible to make some caricature or other out of him, because he was very short in stature and, toward the end, excessively fat. Once again, let us return to the truth, to that literary truth which is ever mindful of human nature and involves a kind of sympathy for everything worthy of it. If we can be just to the erstwhile tinker Bunyan, who in his fanatic visions gave evidence of imaginative power, let us not while doing so crush that amiable and witty creature, that quintessence of soul, that drop of animated wit encased in cotton, Pope. Let us not bully him; as we lead him by the hand to be seated in our medical or (we might say) anatomical chair, let us take care (as though he were still alive) not to make him cry out in pain. In literature I feel we should always accommodate our method to the subject and encompass with particular solicitude anyone who invites and deserves it.

Pope's natural history is quite simple: frail people, they say, are unhappy, and he was twice frail, being delicate in mind and delicate and weak in body; he was doubly irritable. But what grace, taste, and quickness of perception, what consummate accuracy of expression!

Granted, he was precocious. Is that a crime? While still a child, endowed with a sweet look and above all with the sweetest of voices, he was called "the little nightingale." His first teachers didn't amount to much and so he educated himself. At twelve he was learning Latin and Greek at the same time, largely on his own. At fifteen he decided to go to London to study French and Italian in order to be able to read the literature in those languages. His family, Roman Catholics who had retired from trade, were at this juncture living on an estate in Windsor Forest. They regarded their son's desire as a bizarre whim, since from that time on his health would hardly permit him to change his residence. By persisting, he carried his project through. In this way he learned almost everything by himself, making his way as fancy directed him through the various authors and learning his grammar unaided. For recreation he made verse translations of the first passages he came on in the Greek and Latin poets. By sixteen, he said, his taste was as fully formed as it was ever to be.

In all this I see nothing ridiculous, nothing that does not do honor to this fertile young mind. If there is such a thing as the literary temperament, it has never shown itself in anyone in a more distinctive and clearly defined fashion than in Pope. As a general rule, a man is classical by virtue of training and education; but Pope was classical by vocation, so to speak, and by inborn originality. At the same time he was reading the poets he read the best of the critics, preparing himself to add to what they had written. He had an early taste for Homer, whom he read in the original; after Virgil, Statius was his favorite Latin poet. Even then, he already preferred Tasso to Ariosto, a preference he retained ever afterwards.

It was his status as a papist that prevented his being educated in the universities or following the usual paths and methods to learning.

His precocity as an author put him in touch, from his adolescent years, with poets and famous personalities. Dryden, however, who died in May, 1701 [1700], when Pope was twelve, he saw but once. Yet this wonderful child had formed such a lofty and cherished conception of the poet by reading his work that he got some friends to take him into the coffee house which Dryden frequented, whence he returned happy at having seen him. He could now say, like Ovid, *Virgilium vidi tantum* . . . ["I at least saw Virgil . . ."]. Pope always spoke of that illustrious forerunner with profound reverence and never with the least suggestion of being his rival. "I learned the whole art of verse," he said, "merely from reading Dryden's works, and he himself would doubtless have brought that art to its last perfection, if he had been less governed by necessity."[1] Pope had that characteristic trait of literary natures, the faithful worship of genius.

If he hated stupid authors and malicious poets excessively, he admired the good and great ones only the more. The spirits of Malherbe and Boileau were united in him, a bold and novel importation into so free a country.

During his childhood Pope was exposed to many perils and more than once in danger of death by accident or as a result of his constitutional frailty, and there remain testimonies to his tender and lasting gratitude toward those who interested themselves in his welfare or contributed to his preservation. Whatever may be said of his critical irritability and the regrettable excesses to which it carried him, his was a benevolent spirit made for friendship. Some

1. Sainte-Beuve paraphrases Pope's remark recorded in Joseph Spence's *Anecdotes of Books and Men*, ed. S. W. Singer (London, 1820), p. 280.

facts brought to light after his death, for the purpose of blackening his character, have since been explained to his honor, and the totality of his work speaks in his favor.

Counseled by his friend the poet Walsh, whom he met when he was about fifteen, he felt that after all that had been done in poetry only one road to excellence remained open to him. "There have been several great geniuses up to now," Walsh said to him, "but we have not yet had a great poet who was also correct; you be that poet." [2] Pope followed this advice, and his whole fifty-six years were consecrated to that noble study and aim, which he fully accomplished.

Can the pains he took, despite wretched health, to equip himself for this arduous and immortal task be held against him as a fault? Oh, yes, he was all attention, even in conversation, and whenever a thought or a happy, delicate, or lively expression was dropped in his presence or popped into his mind, he was in great haste to get it down on paper. Ever anxious for the best and the most excellent, bit by bit he hoarded up examples, never willingly allowing a particle to be lost. He wore himself out in the process. When necessary, he would get up during the night, and, since he could not manage by himself, awaken his servants, even in winter, in order to write down some thought which he was afraid of losing and which would have slipped out of his mind by morning. For not a few of our best thoughts are drowned and forever sunk from sight between two periods of sleep, like the Egyptians in the Red Sea. We may smile, if we wish, at this excessive concern, at this feverish and parsimonious curiosity, but smile indulgently, as becomes spirits humanized by literary pursuits, who have felt the sweet mania ourselves. Let us not employ a double standard.

You admire Balzac; you quote him more than once and gladly bring him into your discussion of these English authors, where he has no business being. Let me therefore cite him as an example well known to you. I recall one day hearing some interesting revelations about his extraordinary preoccupation and about his authorial egoism when engaged in composition. How often, in the middle of the night, did Balzac not suddenly appear at the bedside of Jules

2. Paraphrased from Spence, *Anecdotes*, p. 280.

Sandeau,[3] who was then living in the same house, and pitilessly startle him awake, in hot haste to read him something he had just that moment finished writing. For he lived in his work as in Vulcan's cavern, where he labored at his forge and hammered away on the anvil; and during all that time the outside world did not exist for him. If you spoke to him of your mother, sister, or mistress, he would say, "Well, that's fine, but let's get back to reality: What are we going to do about Nucingen, about the Duchess of Langeais?" He had turned life inside out; for him the reality was the dream. One day when Jules Sandeau returned from his native region where he had suffered a cruel loss in the death of his sister, Balzac, seeing him again and starting to ask after his family, suddenly said, as though changing his mind, "Well, enough of this chatter, let's get back to serious matters." He meant getting back to work, to *Père Goriot*, I believe it was.

As inspiration and creative zest, this will perhaps be thought splendid; at least it is original, and we should admire in it a unique and powerful capacity for transmutation. Well and good! as we leave this blind and slightly hazy order of creation and condescend to enter into the serene and temperate sphere of moral ideas, of sound and lucid thinking and of elevated and refined meditation, which are properly the object and quarry (as Montaigne would say) of philosophers and sages, let us not make too much sport of this inquisitive and amiable Pope for having harkened to the voice of *his* daemon, *his* genius, for having lent a willing ear to the purely abstract and intellectual inspirations which arise in the solitude of the study or in conversation with a friend during a stroll down some lane in Tibur or Tusculum.[4] And if the mind, while yet remaining calm, feels itself stirred by the rivalry or gentle contradiction of a friend, we need not be shocked, if Pope himself, as a more or less ingenious way of letting us in on his constant preoccupation with literature, confides in us as follows [in Spence's *Anecdotes*]:

3. Léonard Silvain Julien Sandeau (1811–83) was a minor novelist and playwright.

4. Tibur and Tusculum were towns near Rome, celebrated by Cicero and Horace for their scenic beauty, where wealthy Romans built summer villas.

When Swift and I were once in the country for some time together, I happened one day to be saying, "that if a man was to take notice of the reflections that came into his mind on a sudden as he was walking in the fields, or sauntering in his study, there might be several of them perhaps as good as his most deliberate thoughts."—On this hint, we both agreed to write down all the volunteer reflections that should thus come into our heads, all the time we staid there. We did so: and this was what afterwards furnished out the maxims published in our miscellanies. Those at the end of one volume are mine; and those in the other Dr. Swift's.

Such things are ingenious pastimes, the kind of games intellectuals and literary men play. A far cry from Shakespeare or even from Milton, no doubt—but in none of it do I see anything to invite so much ridicule; and in a history of literature, literary diversion, properly so called, even in its more calculated and artificial aspects, has, it seems to me, a rightful claim to indulgent treatment. In like fashion, strictly speaking, Pliny the younger and Tacitus, chancing to spend some time together in the villa at Lake Como or in that house at Laurentium of which we have a lively description, might for several weeks have tried their wits at philosophy and ethics. The great age of inspiration has passed; the sedate age of decline still allows for many amenities and even (as Tacitus and Swift have proven) for true eloquence.

On the subject of Pope, I still have more than one thing to say that I believe worth saying. This name which represents moral poetry, "correct" poetry embellished with all the charm of its polished diction, quite obviously provides me with an occasion and pretext to argue the case for a certain threatened point of view which people nowadays too much despise, having at an earlier time praised it exclusively. The historical point of view has invaded the entire kingdom of letters and will henceforth predominate in every study and preside over all reading. It is not in this regard that I quarrel with M. Taine's book; it is rather that I require of him a supplement, and a few correctives for the future. This book of bold and original criticism is like a tree growing in rich earth that thrusts all its branches toward the bias and favor of Anglo-Saxon vigor. From this viewpoint Pope's poetry is bound to look like an abortive branch because of all English poetry it is the least Anglo-Saxon. But that is no reason for treating it disparagingly.

My general position would be that we ought to combine our efforts, not setting ourselves in mutual opposition or tearing anything down. By virtue of your talent, you invite and oblige us to march at your side toward the great, the powerful, the difficult, toward what without you we should never have entered upon to so great an extent. But, at the same time, do not suppress our pleasant habitual walks, our Windsor landscapes and Twickenham gardens. Let us increase our holdings in the high valleys and the great plateaus, but let us also keep our smiling domains.

In short, take care not to justify that pessimist who again only yesterday was telling me: "The time is not good for Pope, and it is about to become bad for Horace."

It should be clearly understood that in emphasizing, deliberately and by way of example, Pope's merits, I am taking only indirect exception to M. Taine's work. He has in fact recognized all the fine qualities and salient characteristics of that splendid talent and one could even borrow some of his sentences for defining them; only he does not treat this poet as he has treated the other great poets he has encountered up to this point. He does not delight to restore him to his peculiar milieu; on the whole, he rather depresses him, and when he cannot help recognizing a merit in him, fails to represent it in its best light.

I stress this point because the danger today lies in sacrificing literatures and poets that I shall call moderate. For a long time these were favored with all the honors. The special pleas had to be made for Shakespeare, Milton, Dante, and even for Homer, not for Virgil, Horace, Boileau, Racine, Voltaire, Pope, and Tasso, writers long received and recognized by all. Today, the first group is completely triumphant and the situation is entirely reversed. The greatest writers (and the primitives) reign in triumph; those second to them even in inventiveness, but ingenuous and original in thought and expression, the Regniers and Lucretiuses, are restored to their just rank; and it is the moderates, the cultivated and refined writers, the ancient classics, whom we tend to subordinate and whom, if we are not careful, we are inclined to treat somewhat disdainfully.

Relatively speaking, a kind of contempt and scorn has very nearly overtaken them. It seems to me that there is good reason to preserve everything and sacrifice nothing, and while paying full homage and reverence to the great human forces which, like the natural powers they resemble, burst out with a certain alien and uncouth quality, not to cease honoring those other more restrained powers which are less volcanic in expression and adorn themselves in elegance and good nature.

On the day when a critic appears who has M. Taine's profound and lively historical feeling for letters, and like him sinks his roots to the very wellsprings while also thrusting his verdant branches toward the sun—a critic who at the same time does not slight, rather, say, reveres and breathes in, the delicately perfumed flowers of the Popes, Boileaus, and Fontanes—on that day the perfect critic will have been found and the two critical schools reconciled. But I am demanding the impossible: this is plainly a dream.

In the meanwhile, Pope remains a true poet and with all his physical defects one of the finest and noblest literary natures properly so called that has yet been seen. Today, I know, it is hard to approach him except with a good many objections. In the first place he translated Homer—travestied him, it is said. And thereupon Pope is annihilated, placed on the same level with La Motte.[5] Pointing to two or three passages in the original, his detractors enjoy a facile triumph over him. Notice that one is sure in advance of gaining more or less the same victory over every translator of Homer, whoever he may be. To be fair, it must first be said that Pope had a perfect understanding and admiration of Homer; that his preface to the translation is an excellent piece of criticism for its time and still well worth reading today; that the grandeur, the invention, and the fertility of the original, that vast primal universality whence each literary genre has subsequently sprung, are admirably comprehended. The method of translating in rhyming verses is, in Pope's execution, one of supreme elegance, which is in itself a betrayal of Homer. The rhyme led him into phrasal contrasts, antitheses reiterated within the compass of short sentences, the kind of thing

5. Antoine Houdar de La Motte (1672–1731), though ignorant of Greek, published a tasteless French version of the *Iliad*.

Pope does best but which is contrary to the broad Homeric manner, that full natural river with its free-flowing waves, sustained, wide-spreading, and sonorous. Moreover, it is quite apparent that William Cowper, with his rhymeless verses derived from the some-what strained manner of Milton, succeeded no better for his part in rendering, not the unremitting movement, but the rapidity of the Homeric river.[6] The plain fact is that Homer is untranslatable in verse. It was therefore easy for [Richard] Bentley[7] to say, when he saw Pope's *Iliad*, "You must not call it Homer." Pope's work is not for this reason any the less marvelous an accomplishment in itself, and he who performed it deserves to be spoken of, even on this occasion, with every deference and no little praise. In translating Homer, Pope did display too much artificiality, but there was no artificiality in the sincere emotion he felt when reading him. He observed one day to a friend [Spence]: "I always was particularly struck with that passage in Homer, where he makes Priam's grief for the loss of Hector, break out into anger against his attendants and sons; and could never read it without weeping for the distress of that unfortunate old prince." And then he took the book and in fact tried to read the passage aloud: "Out of my sight, ye wretched, shame of my life. . . ." But he was interrupted by his tears.

No example could furnish better proof than Pope's of how much a deeply felt, delicate critical faculty is an active faculty. One does not have this kind of feeling or perception if one has nothing of one's own to give. This good taste, this sensibility so vibrant and alert, implies a vast imagination behind it. The story goes that the first time Shelley heard the poem *Christabel* recited, at a certain magnificent and terrifying passage he took fright and suddenly fainted. In that swoon his whole poem *Alastor* was already present. No less sensitive in his own way, Pope was unable to read to the

6. I borrow these judgments from one of the finest and most accurate English critics. See the three lectures given at Oxford, *On Translating Homer*, by Mr. Matthew Arnold. On the subject of Pope's translation they represent the finest expression of good taste. [Sainte-Beuve]

7. Bentley, one of the greatest classical philologists of his day, was scorned by Pope and his fellow wits as a heavy-handed pedant.

end of that passage in the *Iliad* without bursting into tears. When a man is that much a critic, it is because he is a poet.

This is well demonstrated in that *Essay on Criticism* which he composed at the age of twenty-one and kept several years under lock and key, a poem which seems to me equal to the *Epistle to the Pisos*, called Horace's "Art of Poetry," and to Boileau's as well. Speaking of Boileau, can I therefore accept that strange judgment of a clever man, that contemptuous opinion which by citing it M. Taine makes his own and does not hesitate to endorse in passing: "There are two sorts of verses in Boileau: the majority of them seem to have been written by a high school student, the rest by a good student of rhetoric"? The witty man in question, M. Guillaume Guizot,[8] has no feeling for Boileau as a poet; I should even go so far as to say that he has no feeling for any poet as a poet. I can understand that all poetry does not consist in craftsmanship; but I do not at all understand how, when the subject is a certain art, one can pay no regard to the art itself and so greatly underrate the consummate practitioners of it. Better suppress all poetry in verse at a simple stroke; otherwise speak with due respect of those who knew its secrets. Boileau was one of that small company. So was Pope. How many shrewd and judicious observations, eternally true, I gather in reading him, and in what brief, concise, elegant form they are expressed, expressed once for all. I instance a few of them that should be quoted in the original:

> In Poets as true genius is but rare,
> True taste as seldom is the Critic's share;
> Both must alike from Heaven derive their light,
> These born to judge, as well as those to write.
>
> . . . . . . . . . . . . . . . . . . . .
> Some have at first for Wits, then Poets past,
> Turned Critics next, and proved plain fools at last.

These lines answer in advance those haughty and vain artists, intolerant of all objection, like some we have known, who, blurring all distinctions, can give but a single definition of the critic: "What

8. François Pierre Guillaume Guizot (1787–1874) wrote several volumes of French and English history.

is a critic? an impotent would-be artist." Every self-conceited artist has been all too ready to use this definition of the critic to his own advantage, and over the years it has resulted in an unchecked licentiousness, an orgy as it were, of talent.

Speaking of Homer and his relation to Virgil, Pope lays down the true line of descent and the true course to be taken by classical talents who remain in the order of the tradition:

> Be Homer's works your study and delight,
> Read him by day, and meditate by night;
> . . . . . . . . . . . . . . . . . . . .
> Still with itself compared, his text peruse;
> And let your comment be the Mantuan Muse.
>   When first young Maro in his boundless mind
> A work t'outlast immortal Rome designed,
> Perhaps he seemed above the critic's law,
> And but from nature's fountains scorned to draw:
> But when t'examine every part he came,
> Nature and Homer were, he found, the same.

Certainly the poetry of secondary periods, ages more polished and refined, has never been better exemplified. The poet-critic even attributes rather too much to Homer when, refuting a phrase Horace used about him,[9] he says what we mistake for a fault or oversight in Homer is perhaps only a stratagem of art:

> Nor is it Homer nods, but we that dream.

The ideal function of the true critic Pope has defined and set forth in various noble and inspired passages * * *:

> A perfect judge will read each work of wit
> With the same spirit that its author writ:
> Survey the whole, nor seek slight faults to find
> Where nature moves, and rapture warms the mind,
> Nor lose, for that malignant dull delight,
> The generous pleasure to be charmed with wit.

Then there is the following fine portrait, the ideal of the genre, which every professional critic should keep framed in his study:

9. *Homer dormitat* [Even Homer sometimes nods], in his *Epistle to the Pisos*.

> But where's the man, who counsel can bestow,
> Still pleased to teach, and yet not proud to know?
> Unbiased, or by favour, or by spite;
> Not dully prepossessed, nor blindly right;
> Though learned, well-bred, and though well-bred, sincere;
> Modestly bold, and humanly severe:
> Who to a friend his faults can freely show,
> And gladly praise the merit of a foe?
> Blest with a taste exact, yet unconfined;
> A knowledge both of books and humankind;
> Generous converse, a soul exempt from pride;
> And love to praise, with reason on his side?

In order to be a good and perfect critic, Pope well knew, it is not enough to cultivate and enlarge one's intellectual powers; one must also constantly purge one's mind of every malignant passion and dubious sentiment. The soul must be kept sound and upright.

No one can have such a lively and tender feeling for the beautiful without being terribly shocked by the foul and the ugly. A capacity for exquisite delight exacts its price. Any spirit so open and so delicately responsive to beauties, to the point of tears as in Pope's case, is bound to be equally sensitive to blemishes, to the point of being nettled and angered by them. The man who gets the keenest pleasure from the fragrance of a rose will be the most offended by bad odors. Thus perhaps no one has ever had so highly developed a capacity to be pained by literary folly as Pope had. Yet how shall we behave toward bad authors, those whom nowadays we dare not call simply fools, most of whom are in fact so exposed to the common intelligence that they are no worse than *half-fools?* Pope, who like so many moralists did not often enough practice what he preached, gives us some excellent maxims on this subject in his *Essay.* He tells us that often the best course is to withhold our criticism and let the fool restrain or indulge himself at his own will.

> Your silence there is better than your spite,
> For who can rail so long as they can write?

Let this stand as a warning to us impatient and irascible souls when we come across one of the tasteless, infatuated perennial authors whom we no longer wish even to name!

Pope sums up his entire theory, which is that of the Virgils, Racines, and Raphaels, all those who in art do not favor pure reality, candor at all costs even if it means coarseness, or power at all costs even if it means violence!

> True wit is nature to advantage dressed,
> What oft was thought, but ne'er so well expressed;
> Something, whose truth convinced at sight we find,
> That gives us back the image of our mind.

He is for selection and against excess, even though it be superfluity of wit or talent:

> For works may have more wit than does 'em good,
> As bodies perish through excess of blood.

All these subtle truths are set forth by Pope in elegant verses and in far fewer words than I use to express them here [in French paraphrase]; for it can be said of Pope as of Malherbe,

> D'un mot mis en sa place enseigna le pouvoir.[10]

But over both Malherbe and Boileau he has the advantage of writing in a language very rich in monosyllables. Moreover, his manner of using these short words shows him to be thoroughly English in style, and I think I can safely say that his vocabulary, although it contains a greater proportion of abstract words than is found in other poets, is formed of the best and purest elements of his native tongue. Pope was also well aware that this attempt at literary regularity and an exact codification of taste was something new, unused and long unheard of in his country. In France, he wrote,

> The rules a nation, born to serve, obeys;
> And Boileau still in the right of Horace sways.
> But we, brave Britons, foreign laws despised,
> And kept unconquered, and uncivilized;
> Fierce for the liberties of wit, and bold,
> We still defied the Romans, as of old.

10. "[He] taught the power of a well-placed word." Boileau, *Art poétique*, 1, line 133.

At least until that moment and before Dryden, this was still true. He closes the *Essay* by modestly saying that his Muse will be

> Content, if hence th'unlearned their wants may view,
> The learned reflect on what before they knew—

a thought expressed, according to him, in a single line of excellent Latin worthy of Horace:

> *Indocti discant, et ament meminisse periti.*[11]

In my account of this *Essay* on the art of the critic and poet, I have neglected to mention some delightful models of imitative versification with which the author was able to complement his doctrines so skillfully that the precept provides the example within itself. Among others, there is a famous passage which is perhaps the most perfect example of its kind in modern literature; Addison quoted it with praise in the 253rd number of his *Spectator*:

> 'T is not enough no harshness gives offense,
> The sound must seem an echo to the sense:
> Soft is the strain when Zephyr gently blows,
> And the smooth stream in smoother numbers flows;
> But when loud surges lash the sounding shore,
> The hoarse, rough verse should like the torrent roar:
> When Ajax strives some rock's vast weight to throw,
> The line too labors, and the words move slow;
> Not so, when swift Camilla scours the plain,
> Flies o'er th'unbending corn, and skims along the main.

Bits of this kind, it is understood, are untranslatable; and when Delille, with all his cleverness imitating this passage in the fourth book of *L'Homme des champs*, would tell us to

> Peignez en vers légers l'amant de Flore;
> Qu'un doux ruisseau murmure en vers plus doux encore,[12]

he misses from the outset both the definiteness and the sobriety of Pope, who says simply "Zephyr" and not "Flora's lover." To

11. "Those untaught may learn, and the expert enjoy being reminded."

12. "Paint Flora's lover in light verses; / Let a soft brook murmur in verses still softer." Jacques Delille (1738–1813) published a French translation of *Paradise Lost*.

appreciate Pope at his true value you must read this passage in the original. Pope is no more to be confused with Delille than Gresset is with Dorat.[13] The case is the same as with wines; they all have their several bouquets, and a given bouquet that is nothing much in itself may be everything to a good taste.

I have no intention, obviously, of running through Pope's principal works. What I wish to point out * * * is that if he is not a universal poet in the sense that most strikes us today, he is nonetheless a true poet, although of an order less tempestuous, less impassioned, less glaring, in a mode ornate, correct, and chaste. In the range of his ideas he is much superior to Boileau, as well as in his taste for the picturesque; yet some of the same reproaches have been made against him that I myself, in youthful impertinence, leveled against Boileau at the start of my career.[14] A poet who felt obliged to put out an edition of Pope, or at any rate wrote a preface for it, the Reverend Mr. Bowles, one of the precursors of the English romantic movement, quarreled a great deal with his author and reproached him for many failings. "The true poet," Bowles said, "must have an eye vigilantly familiar with every change of season, with every variation of light and shade in nature, every rock and tree—nay, with every leaf on its most hidden branch. Whoever lacks an eye formed to take notice of every object and cannot at a glance distinguish every diversity of hue and shading will for that reason alone be proportionately lacking in one of the most essential qualifications of a poet."[15] Pope is certainly not lacking in the picturesque; he had a feeling for nature, which he loved and described in his "Windsor Forest." Condemned by poor health to a sedentary life and unable to travel to places celebrated for their natural beauty, he relished the rustic nature offered by the fresh and

13. Jean-Baptiste-Louis Gresset (1709–77) gained fame by his verse tale of a parrot, *Vert-Vert*. Claude-Joseph Dorat (1734–80) was a minor and not very successful dramatist and versifier.

14. See "Boileau" (1829) in *Portraits littéraires*, in which Sainte-Beuve accused Boileau of a too great attention to trivialities in his theory of style and of laboriously fabricating metaphors in his verse.

15. This quotation is a rather loose paraphrase of a passage in Bowles's 1806 edition of Pope's works. William Lisle Bowles (1762–1850) was attacked by Byron for his grudging estimate of Pope's moral and poetic character.

smiling countryside surrounding him. He even drew and painted the landscape, having taken lessons for a year and a half from his friend Jervas. One day he was asked, "Which of the two arts gives you the greater pleasure, poetry or painting?" "I can't exactly say," he answered; "both have a great deal of charm." It is certain, however, that he was far from fulfilling the detailed program Bowles lays down for the poet and the necessary pictorial conditions he requires, which only Wordsworth has since lived up to. Bowles himself wrote some delightful and highly colorful sonnets in this kind and had no hesitation in erecting his personal taste and talent into a law and general theory; as often happens, he took himself for a model.

Let us not confound genres and individual natures; let us not ask of one organization of temperament that which is the peculiar fruit of another. And to Pope let us apply his own eminently just precept:

> In every work regard the writer's end,
> Since none can compass more than they intend.

Friend of Bolingbroke and Swift, Pope did not completely embrace their philosophy in all its boldness. In turning Bolingbroke's ideas into verse by combining them with those of Leibnitz, he did not go beyond a benevolent and enlightened deism. The *Essay on Man*, such as it issued from his hand, with its creditable though incomplete extent and its ornate solemnity, has for a long time belonged to French literature, made available to us by Fontanes's translation and the fine preface he wrote for it. How many accurate definitions and proverbial lines has it yielded! But the *Essay on Man* is not the Pope I prefer. Where he excelled in originality and without going beyond his own true field of observation was in his moral epistles, and M. Taine has rightly called our attention to the one, among others, in which he treats the "characters" and the "ruling passion" of men.[16] After the fashion of La Bruyère, but with the added burden and embellishment of rhyme, Pope here constantly compresses "the greatest amount of thought into the smallest space": that is the essence of his style.

By a series of examples and skillfully chosen observations, this epistle shows us that for anyone who wishes to understand an

16. The first of the *Moral Essays*, addressed to Lord Cobham.

individual man completely, all the evidence is deceptive. All is subject to misinterpretation: his appearance as well as his habits, his opinions as well as his manner of speaking. Even his deeds often belie their motives. Deception can be avoided only by discovering his secret motive, his "ruling passion," provided he has one. Therein lies the key to the whole man. And in a series of examples Pope shows us how each man as he grows older becomes increasingly faithful to this secret mold, which survives everything else and, unmasking itself with the passing of the years, is the last thing about us to be quenched, stamping its seal, as it were, on our expiring sigh.

> Time, that on all things lays his lenient hand,
> Yet tames not this; it sticks to our last sand.
> Consistent in our follies and our sins,
> Here honest Nature ends as she begins.

* * * Pope was completely the poet of his moment, a period at once restrained and brilliant, a memorable era in which English society, without abjuring itself as it did under Charles II, entered upon a regular intercourse with the Continent and lent itself to a useful and noble commerce of thought and manners. Pope is what is called an enlightened spirit. He was formed for choice friendships and these were not lacking to him. How much care and elegance he expended on his epistolary exchanges is apparent in his works; he adapted the diction and tone of his letters to his correspondents. His letters do not seem to me to have been collected and published as they deserve. * * *

Pope's judgments of authors, his conversation on all subjects, especially on literary matters, is marked by an exquisite truthfulness. Chaucer, Spenser, Cowley, Milton, even Shakespeare—he speaks of them all in the most delightful way, putting his finger on the peculiar quality of each talent with impartial good taste. To appreciate the Pope of intimate conversation you must read Spence's *Anecdotes*.

In all the foregoing I wished only to show that it is possible to speak of Pope with affection and sympathy. * * *

*Nouveaux lundis*, VIII, 103–32 (May 30, June 6, and June 13, 1864).

# Selected Bibliography

BABBITT, IRVING. "Sainte-Beuve." In *Masters of Modern French Criticism.* Boston: Houghton Mifflin Co., 1912.

DE GOURMONT, RÉMY. "Sainte-Beuve, créateur de valeurs." In *Promenades philosophiques.* Paris: Société du Mercure de France, 1904.

DEMOREST, J. J. "Sainte-Beuve et Pascal." *PMLA,* LXVIII (1953), 961–74.

GIRAUD, VICTOR. *Port-Royal de Sainte-Beuve.* Les Chefs-d'oeuvres de la littérature expliqués, no. 20. Paris, n.d.

——— "Sur Sainte-Beuve." In *Maîtres d'autrefois et d'aujourd'hui.* Paris: Librairie Hachette, 1914.

LEHMANN, A. G. *Sainte-Beuve: A Portrait of the Critic, 1804–1842.* Oxford: Clarendon Press, 1962.

MACCLINTOCK, LANDER. *Sainte-Beuve's Critical Theory and Practice after 1849.* Chicago: University of Chicago Press, 1920.

MARKS, EMERSON R. "Sainte-Beuve's Classicism." *French Review,* XXXVII (1964), 411–18.

MORE, PAUL ELMER. "The Centenary of Sainte-Beuve." In *Shelburne Essays.* 3d ser. New York: Houghton Mifflin Co., 1905.

MOREAU, PIERRE. *La critique selon Sainte-Beuve.* Paris: Société d'Edition et d'Enseignement Supérieure, 1964.

TURNELL, MARTIN. "Literary Criticism in France." In *Critiques and Essays in Criticism,* ed. R. W. Stallman. New York: Ronald Press, 1949.

VIGGIANI, CARL A. "Sainte-Beuve (1824–1830), Critic and Creator." *Romanic Review,* XLIV (1953), 263–72.

WELLEK, RENÉ. "Sainte-Beuve." In *The Age of Transition.* Vol. 3 of *A History of Modern Criticism, 1750–1950.* New Haven: Yale University Press, 1965.

# Index

159